Manicuring & Pedicuring Mastery

Enhancing Your Mani/Pedi Mastery

JANET McCORMICK

Olympus Story House

Table of Contents

Dedication

To my better half, my identical twin, Jane Seiling, a talented and celebrated author, who has always been there for me in good and bad times. Being an identical twin is incredibly special. Everyone should be so lucky!

Foreword

by Jan Arnold

"Janet McCormick is deeply dedicated to excellence in the nail care profession, specializing in safe and professional practices within salon environments. She is recognized as one of the positive change-makers in the professional nail care industry.

With university degrees in health management and education, coupled with two professional licenses in aesthetics and nail care and 40+ years of experience in the industry, Janet offers a distinctive perspective that goes beyond the nail plate. She views the entire hand, arm, feet, and legs as opportunities not only for beautification but also for the prevention of long-term discomfort and the promotion of wellness.

Her unwavering commitment to the success of professionals in salons drives her efforts to enhance their knowledge and foster a dedication to proficiency and excellence. Janet's principles are firmly grounded in scientific evidence and best practices, ensuring that she never compromises the quality of professional care. She adeptly combines the concept of a nail technician working towards professionalism and a truly accomplished nail professional who embodies excellence and prioritizes preventive care.

In this book, you will discover valuable insights rooted in fact and experience that will empower you and elevate your status as a professional, assuring your clients that they are in caring and capable hands.

Embrace the wisdom shared within these pages of this book: 'Manicure and Pedicure Mastery' and carry the spirit of Janet McCormick into your daily practice as a professional. May we all aspire to be as accomplished and passionate."

Jan Arnold
Co-founder and Style Director of CND
Vista, CA

Jan Arnold is the brains and beauty behind the CND brand, and transformed the family-founded company into a cult professional line that is recognized and utilized with pride internationally by top nail technicians. She has been the champion and advocate of nail technicians her entire 40+ years in the industry and believes education is the foundation of excellence as a successful nail technician.

Preface

by: Janet McCormick

Times have changed, but the focus of nail care has not. Until now.

Our overall world has changed in life, business, everything, since I joined this industry 40+ years ago – 1979… but manicures and pedicures are still the same as they were in Cleopatra's time. The nail care industry is still performing the same protocol as way back then! Manicuring & Pedicuring Mastery is changing that.

My personal journey to authoring this book did not begin with an overwhelming desire to upgrade these services. It began when I went back to beauty school to add a license in esthetics to my service repertoire. Then, one day I had a palm-to-head epiphany, saying to myself, "manicures and pedicures need the same results as facial care, and they can!" I pursued this thought by upgrading my salon manicure and pedicure protocols to skin care-based protocols and passing them on to other dual licensed professionals who also had an "aha!" moment, and here they are.

I believe understanding and using the concepts of this book and taking the information and protocols into manicuring and pedicuring services can take a nail care career to a higher level, as well as enhancing the professional's income. Even if you perform other specialties, such as enhancements, nail art and more, you can upgrade your services to support the client's skin as a beautiful frame around your work while enhancing your income. It did for me and for many other nail professionals, and I also wish it for you.

Janet McCormick, MS, CIDESCO
For further questions concerning the information in this book, contact Janet at janet.mccormick.info@gmail.com. See www.nailcare-academy.com/about for more information on this author. For a discussion concerning the information in this book, contact Janet at janet.mccormick.info@gmail.com

Chapter 1

Changes in Manicures and Pedicures

Many nail professionals feel marginalized within the professional beauty industry, and in many ways, they are. Other beauty professionals often underestimate the complexity of manicuring skills and express this belief openly. For instance, although most cosmetology courses offer only a few hours of education in manicuring and require minimal practice services, cosmetologists may claim, "anyone can do a manicure," and assert their ability to perform excellent services.

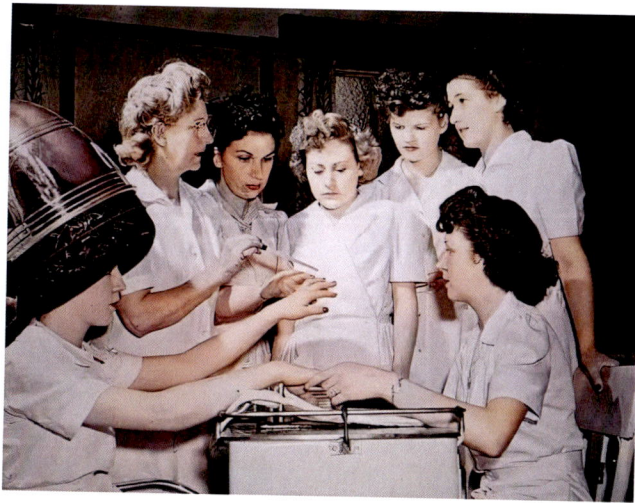

Teaching Manicures in school in early days. Not much has changed!

Hair designers extend this sentiment to pedicures as well, suggesting that "a pedicure is merely a manicure on the feet," and implying that no special training is needed beyond their brief manicure instruction. While some may indeed perform these services competently, those who receive praise for manicuring seek specialized training and take pride in their expertise. Conversely, hair designers who have only their usual training occasionally offer mini-manicures that often reveal their limited training through their work.

Historically, manicure service pricing was influenced by the industry's perception of the service as an add-on to hair treatments, typically performed during the client's time under the hair dryer hood. These services were rarely comprehensive, often amounting to little more than a polish change due to time constraints. Consequently, prices were set low to align with the add-on concept, and clients later expected similar pricing for full-service stand-alone manicures. As a result, pricing failed to reflect the actual cost of products and time—referred to as 'scheduled units'—for complete natural nail services provided by specialists.

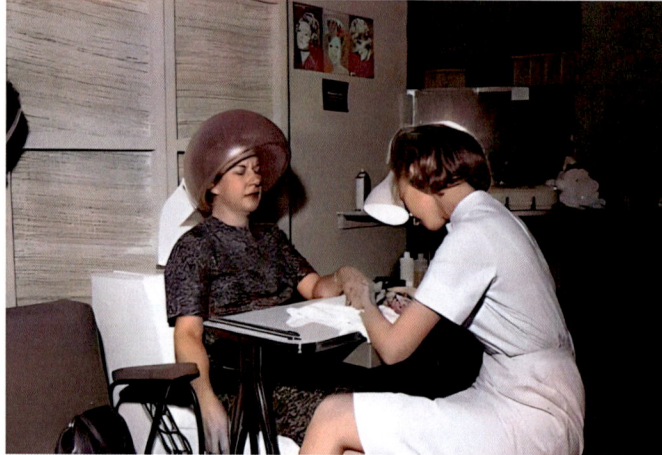

Manicures were given while the client was under the hair dryer.

Manicure services were defined as one service, a manicure, on the salon menu, leading to perceptions of them as "just manicures," which kept prices low. Clients would request a manicure, and upon visiting the salon, they received a basic nail cleanup, not a full manicure. The only enhancement available for these menu-driven services was a brief paraffin treatment performed concurrently with other tasks.

The spa manicure, an extended service introduced in the nineties typically requires 45 minutes to an hour and a half, and includes additional treatments. It could not be easily incorporated as a upgrade due to the typical half-hour scheduling of basic manicures. This service could only be booked for a subsequent visit unless the nail professional had an opening.

This pervasive "just a manicure" mindset not only fostered low-cost expectations for manicure services but also resulted in lower profit margins per time unit for nail departments compared to other salon or spa services. This led to reduced earnings for nail professionals, who often earned less than their peers in other beauty disciplines. Additionally, it engendered a lack of respect for the service among other beauty professionals and salon owners, and potentially for the nail professionals themselves.

Pricing Changes

In the 80s, manicures cost $10-12 in full-service salons, a price point carried over to new nail specialty salons. Pedicures were rare, and when available, cost $15-$20.

Now, early 2024 surveys reveal that manicures start at $22-25 while pedicures start at $35-$125 for a basic half-hour maintenance session, with prices ranging up to $150-$175 and beyond for custom or treatment pedicures by specialists.

What are your current charges? Natural nail services are increasingly valued as essential personal care by both men and women, and pedicurists are gaining recognition for their expertise.

In the 80s and 90s, the popularity of artificial nails temporarily boosted nail professionals' incomes. However, this increase plateaued due to competition from budget salons offering discounted services. Despite their passion for their craft, nail professionals faced ongoing challenges in achieving financial success.

One of the first innovations after acrylic nails became popular was the white-tipped French Manicure

Finally, changes for nail professionals

When acrylic nails gained popularity, nail professionals often avoided performing manicures due to their low profitability. However, the world of manicuring has evolved significantly over the past two decades, with prices for natural nail services increasing. This shift began in the mid-90s when the 'natural' look returned to vogue, and manicures found a new home on spa nail tables. Day spas played a pivotal role in reviving these services, aligning them with the pampering ethos of the spa environment, where the pungent odor of acrylic nails was unwelcome.

Pedicures followed a distinct trajectory in their pricing development, yet their rapid price escalation also influenced manicure pricing. Despite their centuries-old history, pedicures were unknown in America or seldom considered. They languished at the bottom of service menus in the few salons that offered them, and many, including nail salons, had removed them entirely from their offerings in the 80s due to unprofitable pricing.

The debut of luxurious throne-style pedicure chairs by European Touch in Milwaukee, WI, followed by CND's Marine SpaPedicure line from Vista, CA, empowered spas to reintroduce these services as novel and exceptional spa offerings. These innovations justified setting higher prices that more accurately reflected the costs, time investment, professional compensation, and product expenses.

European Touch, Milwaukee, Wisconsin, developed the first Pedicure chair in 1985

Creative Nail Design (now, CND), Vista, California, developed the first complete product line for pedicures in 1995. The line is credited with quickly launching pedicures to the top spa service requested in spas in the US for several years.

Fortunately, the increased prices were validated by strong demand for the service. Pedicures became the fastest-growing spa service for over five years and have remained a top choice since 2000. As a result, nail professionals saw improved earnings, and nail departments became more profitable. With the rise of spa pedicures, the prices for both basic and spa manicures also increased, benefiting all parties involved.

Show your toes!

In the 80s, exposed toes were a rarity, reserved for special occasions. Today, sandals are a year-round fashion staple, and flaunting one's toes has become not just acceptable but fashionable. Displaying vibrant colors and nail art is now a style statement, with unadorned nails seen as a fashion faux pas.

In 2005, Allure Magazine observed that "pedicures have become a lifestyle service, appointed more frequently than haircuts." This marked a significant transformation within a decade. In 2023, W Magazine described pedicures as "arguably one of the most beloved beauty treatments, a common delight for beauty enthusiasts and casual visitors alike."

In the 90s, the introduction of higher-priced spa manicures and pedicures marked a significant shift in the burgeoning spa trend…. The combination of a spa manicure and pedicure into a package with no other services became known as a 'mini package,' a sought-after indulgence.

Fashionistas now proudly show their toes. Pedicures are credited with bringing toes into the light of day.

In the 90s, the introduction of higher-priced spa manicures and pedicures marked a significant shift in the burgeoning spa trend. Spa gift packages emerged as a popular offering, designed to provide high-end relaxation experiences for gift recipients. These packages have remained a top choice for gift-giving, with salons quickly adopting this lucrative addition to their services. The packages typically include a series of treatments performed consecutively, often accompanied by lunch and a special beverage, enhancing the luxury and pampering aspect. The combination of a spa manicure and pedicure became a staple in spas and salon.

These luxury packages not only introduced new clients to spa manicures and pedicures but also converted many into regular patrons. Style-conscious clients began to view the mani/pedi not as a mere luxury but as an essential part of their monthly beauty maintenance. The demand shifted from basic manicures to the more elaborate luxury services.

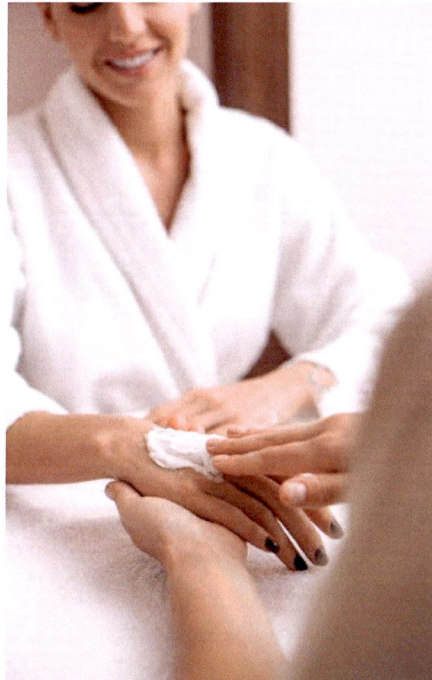

Spa manicures and pedicures are established as lifestyle services for many women.

The increasing popularity of pedicures led to the emergence of a new specialty within the nail industry: the pedicurist. In 1999, as a spa director in a large spa system. The author employed a manicurist who expressed a desire to specialize in pedicures and be recognized as 'a pedicurist.' This marked the beginning of a recognized specialty that has since become established in the beauty industry. With the rising prices for pedicures, these specialists now rank among the highest earners in salon settings.

Expanding manicures and pedicures

Until the early 2000s, basic manicure protocols had remained unchanged for millennia. The introduction of enhancements had revolutionized the industry, yet manicures had seen little innovation. The 1990s saw the addition of the spa manicure, which included a mask and possibly paraffin, but it was not until the turn of the century that spas began to offer extended manicures and pedicures featuring a variety of products and treatments. These services often reflected the spa's theme and were marketed as 'signature' treatments to denote their exclusivity and unique design. For instance, a Florida spa might offer a Signature Citrus Spa Manicure and Pedicure, incorporating citrus-scented products and complementing beverages like fruit juices or a Mimosa.

Spas and upscale salons started to craft specially named manicures and pedicures to align with seasons, holidays, or the spa's branding. A Valentine's Day package, for example, might feature a Chocolate Cherry Cordial Valentine Manicure and Pedicure, complete with chocolate-scented products and a small box of themed candies for the client. Seasonal offerings, such as Harvest Manicures and Pedicures, would include autumnal scents like pumpkin and complementary treats like pumpkin bread with cider.

This trend of designing exclusive services has continued to attract new clients and increase service revenue.

Chapter 2

Upgrades in Nail Services

A meaningful change in manicure and pedicure services began when a few nail professionals added esthetics to their repertoire. (Including the author, Janet McCormick, LE, 1994.) These pioneers developed a new perspective on hand and foot care, distinct from their peers.

The esthetics courses emphasize protocols that enhanced facial skin, inspiring these nail professionals to integrate their newfound skincare knowledge into their hand and foot care services. Many switched to skincare-focused products and adapted their service protocols to resemble the facials they learned in esthetician training. As a result, their manicures and pedicures became more treatment-oriented, addressing the skin as well as the nails, leading to noticeable improvements in service outcomes.

Other nail professionals, observing these advancements, adopted the innovative protocols, learning from estheticians and reaping the benefits of this approach. For those prioritizing results-oriented services, their manicure and pedicure skills have significantly evolved with their expanded skincare knowledge.

These skincare-centric manicures and pedicures necessitate a trained nail professional capable of recommending services tailored to improve the skin on the client's hands, arms, feet, and legs. Like facial services in skincare, the nail professionals analyze the skin and suggest suitable treatments. In this new philosophy, client skin analysis guides service customization, focusing on skin health rather than solely on nail aesthetics—though beautifully manicured nails are a happy byproduct.

The "skincare-based manicures and pedicures" protocol is gaining traction in the industry, becoming a preferred method for many nail professionals eager to enhance their client offerings. However, this approach requires nail professionals to be proficient not only in executing these specialized protocols but also in conducting thorough skin and nail analyses.

Proficiency in analysis of the skin and nails of the hands and feet to determine their needs in care is key to success in skincare-based manicures and pedicures

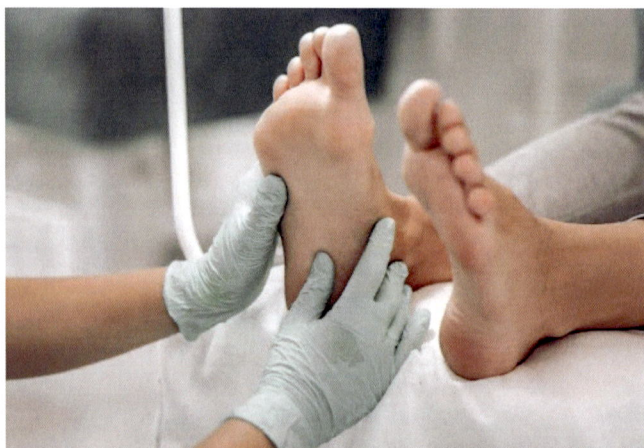

Thorough analysis of the feet is crucial to successful care.

With these advanced manicures and pedicures, professionals can command higher prices, leading to increased earnings in an industry they are passionate about. The industry has evolved, and those willing to embrace these new standards are finding success.

Framing

As this innovative approach to manicures and pedicures progressed, nail professionals performing enhancements noticed the improvements in the skin of clients treated by natural nail specialists. Many adopted the foundational treatments to enhance the skin around their clients' nails, a technique now known as "framing the nails." This concept not only beautifies the nails but also improves the surrounding skin, leading to increased client satisfaction and higher income for the nail professionals.

In framing, skin care treatments are inserted in the services without interfering with the target service. Framing treatments are further discussed in this section.

Comparing the Old to the New

Traditional manicures and pedicures remain the standard curriculum in beauty schools due to the limited hours available for nail education. These programs focus on the essentials required for board examinations, leaving advanced techniques like skin and nail analysis for post-license courses. To illustrate the differences between conventional and skin care-based services, the following chart contrasts the traditional protocol taught in schools with the new skin care-oriented approach:

Traditional Manicure and Pedicure	Skin care-based Manicure and Pedicure
1) Shorten, shape, remove polish	1) Remove polish, observe nails, shorten/ shape
2) Soak	2) Analysis & recommendations
3) Cuticle and callus work	3) Exfoliation massage & traditional massage
4) Mask (optional)	4) Mask and treatment products (optional)
5) Massage	5) Cuticle and callus work
6) Polish prep and polish	6) Polish prep and polish
7) Home care, reappointment, and release	7) Home care, reappointment, and release

The key distinctions between traditional and skin care-based services include:

- A more thorough analysis of the skin and nails on the hands and feet.
- Inclusion of the hands, arms, nails, feet, and legs in the new protocol, such as using a scrub pedicure for scaly winter legs.
- Preparation of the skin for product absorption through scrub exfoliation.
- Earlier massage in the treatment to warm the skin and enhance ingredient penetration.

- Clients relax earlier in the treatment, leading to a more enjoyable experience

- Selection of treatment products tailored to the clients' skin and nail needs.

These advancements elevate the aesthetic services for hands and feet to a treatment focused level, provided the nail professional is adequately educated in skin and nail conditions and improvement methods. Unlike previous protocols that focused on aesthetics and moisturization, these services and the necessary education are the central themes of this book.

Chapter 3

Water - or Not

Another change came for nail professionals open to the new treatment concept for these services: the elimination of soaking the nails on the hands and soaking of the feet. And it fit right into the purpose of the new protocols.

Nail professionals have always soaked their clients' fingernails and feet in water. Soaking has always been thought to be important and the best option to soften the skin, thus allowing the best results for the treatment, and in the meantime, relaxing the client. Few manicures and pedicures were performed without the soak, and in pedicure services, it became a standard with the development of the spa chair.

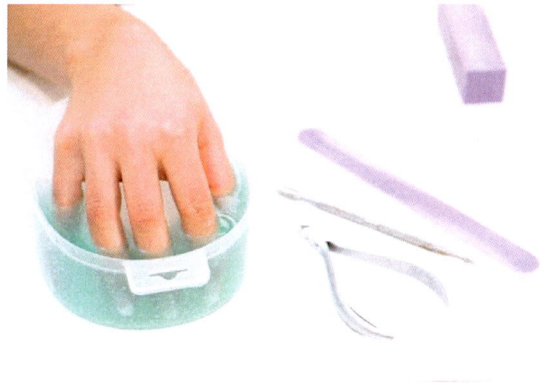

Soaking the nails in a manicure and the full feet in pedicures has been a part of our protocols since manicuring and pedicuring began centuries ago.

Many clients enjoy the bubbles and relaxation of soaking their feet.

This practice began being questioned for several reasons. First, a fingernail is constructed in layers that are structured like fiberboard or fish scales. They are held together by intercellular adhesive materials which stiffen and shape the nails – the healthier the intercellular adhesive, the stronger the nail. However, when in water or other solvents often, these oils and natural adhesives may be softened or damaged, and often cause a condition referred to as layering or peeling (Delamination).

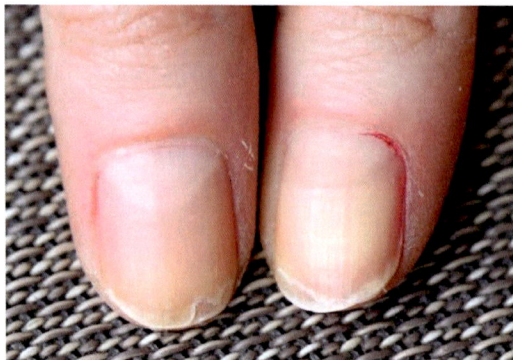

Peeling nails are difficult to correct but can be with careful treatment.

The cause of delamination centers on the natural adhesives failing to hold the nail layers together on the free edge due to water immersion. Water is considered a universal solvent, meaning it will dissolve something when many other solvents will not. But this will not usually happen with the natural adhesives in the nail plates without an additional solvent's help in the water, and alas, nail professionals provide it. When soaking the fingertips, nail professionals usually add something to the water to increase and speed the softening of the nail plate and cuticles (eponychium). Many times, detergent is added because it is effective in dissolving oils – some of us remember Madge, a nail technician soaking her client's nails at her nail table in a Palmolive TV ad. (Other soak products are similar.) Nail plates become weakened by these solvents and that can result in layering, especially with the filing and

12

other manicuring activities that follow, along with the punishment non-gloved hands take at home or at work.

The second reason it began being questioned was the retention of polish on the nails. When the nails are soaked in water, they change shape, become flatter, and become swelled with water. This shape is retained for a time after the polish is applied, according to the health of the nail plate. In the meantime, the polish layers have dried into the shape of the soaked nail and become fully cured in that shape. Then, later, as the nail plate dries, it returns to its natural shape, producing a "pull" on the shape of the cured polish. The polish becomes stressed and susceptible to damage, chipping, and peeling, making it much less durable than the polish on a non-soaked nail.

The third reason for questioning soaking is centered on bloodborne pathogens and the disinfection protocols of the soaking tubs. It is said that 70% of pedicurists were not properly sanitizing and disinfecting their tubs, and it was proven that this lack of proper safety practices caused the injuries and even the death of some salon clients. Performing the soakless protocol eliminates these fears by removing any potential for clients to be exposed to waterborne microbes.

In the early 2000's many deaths and injuries were caused by poor sanitation/disinfection habits for pedicure soaking bowls. Examples of articles about the cases are:

The last reason is time. In manicures, the manicurist must go to the sink for the water and solvent, then clean and sanitize it later. In pedicuring, it is even more complex both in method and the amount of time with quality disinfection taking over ten minutes – the disinfectant usually must soak in the tub for ten minutes, and then there is the pre-cleaning and post service set-up time.

Benefits of Soakless

The soakless protocol is not new—it was first performed in the 90's as a shortcut to manicuring, but it is now more refined, expanded into pedicuring, and goes far beyond the "quicky" attitude. The list of benefits includes more than speed, as follows.

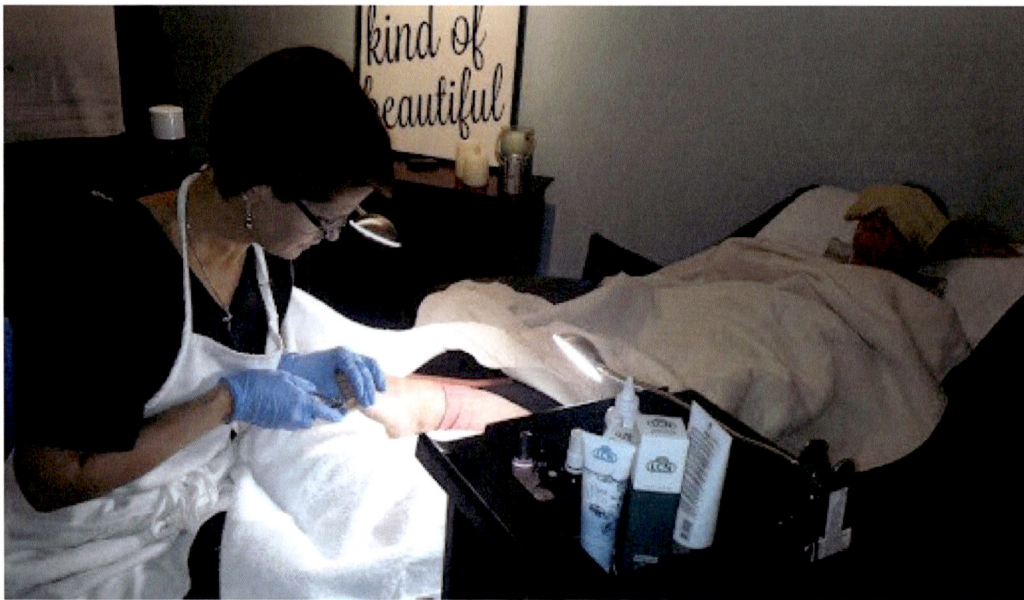

Soakless manicures and pedicures offer many advantages to nail professionals; they are becoming a trend in many salons.

1. The natural nail adhesives are protected from dissolution (see above).
2. The client appreciates three massages, and this replaces the desire for bubbles in the soak. (The cleansing massage, the exfoliating massage, and the traditional massage.)

> Pedicures have no problems with polish coming off or being damaged because they do not suffer the constant abuse and activity fingernails do. Polish on toenails may stay on so long it may grow off. It is even more likely to happen with the soakless pedicure.

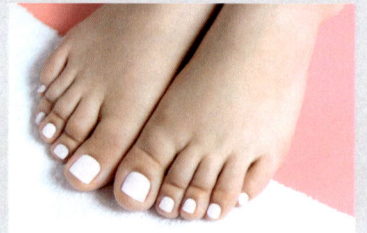

3. The service takes less time due to no fill and emptying time, and the lack of cleansing/disinfection of the soak bowl and the "set time" for disinfection.
4. Polish retention is enhanced due to no softening of the nail plate.
5. Soakless protocols allow more time for pampering the client and prep for the next client.
6. Soakless protocols are much less stressful and fatiguing due to less body movement as during the filling/emptying processes and the disinfection process.
7. State boards love it, removing the necessity for logging disinfection activities. In-the-know boards know it is more hygienic. (Do check with your state boards, though, as some are not up with the times on this, nor have the required knowledge.)
8. Lack of the need for time-consuming disinfection protocols for pedicure bowls alleviates many disinfection products and the time required for "set," allowing more profitability for the salon/professionals.

9. No expensive plumbed chair is needed.

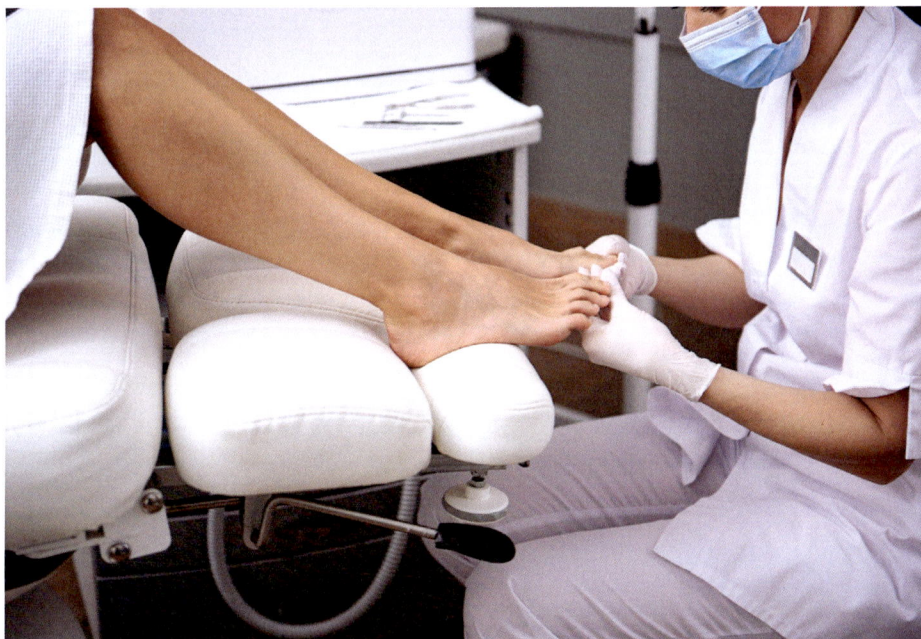

A towel or cover should be over the foot of the chair

10. Physicians and podiatrists are more likely to refer their patients.

Due to the illnesses caused by soaking services, physicians, and podiatrists as well as in-the-know clients openly prefer soakless manicures and pedicures being performed. Those illnesses (some resulting in disability and/or death) are caused by careless disinfection practices of untrained or uncaring nail technicians.

The disabilities and deaths led to states adopting the sanitation and disinfection protocol written originally by the Nail Manufacturer's Council for foot baths plus a log requirement for them. They are now a procedural requirement by most if not all states. Board Inspectors in the states check for the logs during their compliance visits. The link for downloading the procedure is: https://schoonscientific.com/wp-content/uploads/2016/08/Guidelines-for-Cleaning-Manicuring-Equipment_ENG.pdf

Due to the advantages of soakless pedicures, many nail professionals have changed to performing the soakless protocols exclusively in their manicures and pedicures, especially those who accept referrals from and refer to physicians and podiatrists or work in their offices. This trend has caught fire in our industry. (See www.nailcare-academy.com, blog on Soakless Services.) But more importantly, reports of infections and injuries are becoming fewer, and many believe it is due to 1) the better education in prevention of the transfer of disease, and 2) the changes to soakless protocols.

"Soakless," "Waterless," "Dry"

What a nail professional calls this pedicure is their business, of course, but it has been "soakless" since it began to be the pedicure for the author in the 90s. Consider this: It is not waterless. The nail professional performing this protocol uses warm, wet towels on the client in many ways. It is not waterless nor dry. Education while they are a client is the key to their desire to return.

Choose your label for the protocol in how you address it to your clientele. However, in this book, it is the "soakless."

Resistance to Soakless

Some clients resist giving up the soak, however. First, uninformed clients may prefer the whirlpool soak because of the bubbling of the water, the relaxation, aroma, and more. Many nail professionals are not adept at getting clients past this objection initially. The many professionals that have changed over completely to soakless learned to eliminate the objections of their clients quickly.

If clients are resistant to the change to soakless, education is the key to their changeover. Following are the education points for them:

1. Most podiatrists/physicians say there is to be no soaking for clients that have any type of lymphedemas, circulatory problems, or chronic illnesses, such as PAD. Most podiatrists will also say that insulin-dependent diabetics should not be soaked, nor should patients with immune-suppression illnesses.

2. At-risk clients, due to their chronic illness, heal slowly in the case of injury. There must be no chance of exposure to water-borne infections for these clients. If they do become infected with even a minor injury, suffering is a definite result, and death may be the ultimate result.

3. These clients tend to suffer dryness due to their illness and medications, which makes them prone to callusing. This dryness is exacerbated by soaking. Ulcers can develop on these clients beneath calluses where they may become slow or no-healing ulcers that may be deadly for them, especially for diabetics.

The secret to convincing routine clients with no chronic illnesses to change to a soakless pedicure is to tell them there are three massages in the service (the cleansing massage, the exfoliating massage, and the treatment massage) and to suggest they try the new protocol. The nail professional can also mention the dangers of waterborne microbes—they all have heard about the problems, and so most are then convinced.

What a nail professional does with those few clients who continue to reject soakless is their decision. A suggestion is they refer the client to a soaking pedicurist with a hug and an "I will miss you so. You are welcome to come back any time" (emphasis on the latter) and let them go. In the experience of the author, it takes two to three visits to other salons before they call to come back for the soakless protocol. With these and the other changes in your protocols and salon, your "differences" will set you above the salons they change to that soak, and they will be back.

Soakless seemed so very radical when it was introduced, so it faced resistance not only from clients but from nail technicians. Its time has come, however, through education of

Chronic illness is growing in the United States, and performing services on these clients requires special training. But schools are not preparing their students to work safely on these clients. Therefore, it is the graduate nail technician's professional responsibility to seek out further information on performing safe care on these clients.

the nail professionals and clients, as well as the approval of physicians and podiatrists for soakless pedicures to become fully accepted as the norm.

The differences in protocols: soak vs no soak

Some trainers have tried to say performing soakless is difficult, a complex protocol. That is far from the truth. The basic difference between the soakless and the soak manicure/pedicure is in the cleansing/softening protocol. The soak clients soak their fingers/feet at the start of the service; in the soakless protocol, the hands are washed before the service/the nail professional cleanses the feet and then applies a good lotion and cuticle softener and then wraps them in a warm towel or into a thin plastic bag and cloth mitt while prepping the other foot. Also, while soak pedicurists replace the clients' feet in the water to keep them warm between steps, in the soakless, the foot not being treated is wrapped in a warmed towel or placed in terry mitts, and this feels great.

A significant difference between the soak and soakless pedicures is the danger of waterborne microbes that may be present in the water in a soak bath. Yes, the danger is diminished when the technician performs excellent due diligence in cleansing and disinfecting between pedicures, but not only is this very time-consuming to get right, but even the chair manufacturers will say perfection in this safety activity is out of reach. They will not guarantee the danger is alleviated due to the constant occurrence of human error—poor cleaning, etc.

Most clients are aware of this danger but use the "that won't happen to me" excuse that is prevalent in life. They need foot care or want it, so they take the chance. It also means that given the opportunity for soakless, the vast majority will be happy to try soakless and then will stick with it.

The new protocol services in this book are soakless.

Chapter 4

Retention-based New Client Entrance and Seating

These manicures and pedicures, upgrades to traditional services performed by nail professionals, are customized to yield enhanced results, thereby bolstering the client's trust in the nail professional. These services are designed with a greater focus on client retention compared to the conventional same-ole/same-ole protocols.

However, gaining and maintaining trust begins with the professional's approach when the client first enters; it continues throughout the service and into subsequent appointments. The clients must feel that the professional genuinely cares about the health of their hands and feet to remain loyal; they must not perceive the new services as mere tactics to increase revenue or push products.

The decision to return to a salon starts when the client steps into a clean and inviting waiting room. From there, it is up to the reception staff and then the professional to ensure the client's continued patronage. Trust must be established immediately, while the client is in the waiting room, even before they are seated at the professional's station or in the pedicure chair. "It begins with the front staffs' demeanor and attitude towards the incoming clients".

The initial greeting of new clients by the reception staff is a pivotal moment in securing their return. This staff must recognize their role and create a welcoming atmosphere that consistently makes clients feel valued. A genuine smile, eye contact, and acknowledgment are crucial. Then, the clients waiting in the reception area should be approached appropriately by their assigned nail professional and escorted to the nail table or pedicure area in a trained manner that fosters the initial sense of trust.

Good salons and spas have failed due to the poor attitudes of their reception staff.

The impression first offered by the desk receptionist begins the client's decision on whether to return or not to return.

After identifying their client, the nail professional should greet them with a smile, appearing welcoming and enthusiastic. Upon approaching the clients, the nail professional should stand directly in front of them, extending their right hand and leaning slightly forward for a handshake. (Be mindful of clients who prefer not to shake hands and adhere to pandemic restrictions when necessary.) Clients are welcomed by name by the nail professional, who introduces themselves while still smiling. Only after this introduction should they invite the clients to the service area for their scheduled service. **Do not ask, "And what are you here for today?" Always be prepared with the appointment details.**

The process of greeting and accompanying new clients to their stations is crucial as it subtly conveys the nail professional's attitude toward them. It must be welcoming and positive, more than just a greeting followed by a turn to walk to the workstation. Professionals should never turn their backs on clients and lead with "follow me." (The adage goes, "When she can see your back, she won't be back.") Instead, maintain eye contact as much as possible, walking beside them with the body turned slightly toward them (holding any papers in the outside hand). Engage them in conversation during the walk, starting with a question like, "Have you had a [service name] before?" even if it is known they have not had one in this salon or spa. If the client is new to the service, express pleasure in providing their first professional [service name] and assure them of an enjoyable experience. If they have had the service before, inquire about their enjoyment (not where) and promise a pleasant experience today at [salon or spa name]. Discuss the weather only if it is severe; if so, thank them for braving the elements and assure them the visit will be worth it. If the service is a manicure, guide the new client to the hand washing station and instruct them on proper hand and nail washing (using a brush) for each visit.

The professional's manner of greeting a new client sets the tone of the beginning relationship.

Walking the client to the chair with a friendly, professional demeanor shows him or her the professional is committed to their experience, and cares about it being the best possible.

For pedicure services, clients are greeted as described and led to the pedicure area. Assist them as needed while seating, help with shoe removal if it's salon policy, and place the shoes in a designated area during the service.

Other appropriate salon/spa policies include removing jewelry and placing it in a secure location (such as their purse, to be worn after polish application?), offering a cover if the weather is cold, and providing a beverage of choice that the salon offers.

Every initial appointment should be scheduled for an additional 15 minutes compared to repeat appointments to accommodate the New Client Protocol. Subsequent appointments will have

New Client Sheet
It is essential for new clients to complete a NCS, which includes a health survey This is a safety precaution, and a responsible nail professional will always adhere to it. They should review their client's health survey for any chronic illnesses that may preclude soaking. If a condition is indicated that should not be soaked and the salon has spa whirlpool chairs, it is crucial to confirm whether the client has doctor's permission for a whirlpool pedicure; if not, offer a soakless pedicure until they obtain such permission. This also presents an opportunity to educate them about the benefits of soakless pedicures.

routine set times, according to the service being performed. Typically, in follow-up manicure appointments, clients perform hand washing independently, and the analysis by the nail professional is brief but necessary at every visit and should be acknowledged by the client. The client arrives with clean hands, and upon seating, the professional adopts a "palms up" stance to initiate the brief analysis, asking, "How are your hands and nails doing today?" No casual conversation should occur until after this analysis. Hand washing is not required for pedicures, except by the professional or if a manicure follows the pedicure.

Repeat clients should receive the same level of enthusiasm and smiles, and the same escort to the service area. However, if the appointment is with the same nail professional, it should include a personal remark to show recognition. This can be challenging without a system to remember clients until they become regulars. Recognition is significant to clients and may be the deciding factor in their return to the salon or spa, reinforcing their perception that the nail professional cares about them.

One method to ensure client connection is to make a brief note on their card or in the "notes" section of their computer profile to remind the nail professional of personal details for a few appointments. This requires creativity, but nail professionals are adept at quickly establishing such methods. For example, a note like "8-23tr/china" could indicate a trip to China that has either occurred or is upcoming, prompting the professional to inquire about it during the walk to the service area. Another note like "nw.grchd 6-23" might signify a new grandchild expected in June, allowing for a congratulatory comment on this joyous event.

Small things that count

The client/professional relationship in nail care services is intimate due to the physical contact involved. It is often more personal than most other relationships in a client's life. To establish a long-standing, trusted, and meaningful relationship, certain subtle but crucial activities must occur.

1. Eye contact is essential but can be a time killer during services, so it must be used judiciously to establish a connection without hindering the professional tasks at hand. The most critical times for eye contact are during the client's entrance, analysis and consultation, and the closing activities of the services. Practice makes perfect, as nail professionals are busy and eye contact can be easily overlooked. (Also, note that eye contact is not embraced in the culture of many Americans.) With practice, it becomes automatic and even enjoyable in establishing connections with clients. Even if clients do not maintain much eye contact, it is important for the professional to look at them.

2. Friendliness is a significant factor in building clientele. It may seem cliché but compare the experience of a service in a budget salon where time is the highest consideration, and the professional may not speak conversational English. Friendliness is a huge clientele builder. (However, gossip is not friendliness—it can backfire, and focusing too much on the professional's life can damage the relationship.)

3. Their appointed time is theirs. Avoid talking to others when a client is in your chair—clients notice when you are distracted and do not appreciate it, especially if they are new.

4. Stay on time. Clients waiting while their appointment time is used on another client feel undervalued. Practice your timing and get it right!

Clients do not want to wait in the waiting room while another client is being serviced during their purchased time.

5. Provide the service they need, but no more. Your analysis is crucial here. Learn to recognize if a condition requires more time than scheduled and inform the client upfront. For example, excessive callusing may need more time for complete correction for three reasons: 1) aggressive removal may cause soreness, 2) you do not want to rush the necessary removal, and 3) gradual removal (over multiple appointments, if severe) prevents thick recurrence. Then, suggest a second treatment service focused solely on callus removal, explaining that it costs less due to the shorter duration and absence of massage or polishing.

6. If there is extra time, some technicians offer a complimentary upgrade. For instance, if the client's condition is excellent and the service will take less time, offer an upgrade as a thank you for their loyalty, such as a decal during polishing, a heat wrap, or a longer massage. Inform the client that the activity is a free upgrade today due to their diligent home care, which should be acknowledged if it contributes to their condition. Rewards for home care are appreciated by clients, and some may schedule the experienced upgrade for their next appointment and pay for it.

Offering to wax the hair on toes as a bonus service can add a new service for this client's appointments in the future

7. If they consistently maintain excellent condition, consider scheduling less time for them—some salons offer a Maintenance Pedicure at a slightly lower price and duration, but clients must be informed that they need to maintain their condition or revert to the standard, more expensive pedicure. The Maintenance Pedicure is not listed on the menu; it is offered as a reward for good home care and suggested as such. This encourages the continued purchase and use of home care products and optimizes the schedule.

> **Trust through Connection**
> Connection in professional care is not personal; it is the active development of trust by the client of the professional in their care. Connection is vital to client return and the purchase of and following instructions in home care.

These techniques develop a connection (trust) with clients, and if a nail professional internalizes their importance, they become part of their professional behavior. One reason clients switch salons is the lack of a developed connection with the technicians. Understanding connection and its role in trust-building is crucial for growing and maintaining a clientele.

Chapter 5

At the table/chair: Analysis/Consultation

After the initial entrance and seating, skincare-based professionals adopt a new philosophy of care. This philosophy is applied at every appointment, although as clients become more familiar with the process, the time spent, and the extent of the discussion may decrease. Clients will anticipate this care, instinctively adopting the appropriate posture for their treatment—palms up for manicures and feet positioned on the footrest or in the foot care area for pedicures, signaling readiness for the examination.

The practice of conducting a thorough analysis distinguishes a professional from their peers. In time, this activity will become a benchmark for evaluating professionals across different salons and spas, with this step being recognized as a hallmark of these nail professionals. It leaves a lasting impression. The act of performing an analysis not only elevates the service provided by nail professionals in a salon or spa but also becomes a point of comparison for clients who may visit other establishments and notice its absence.

Nail professionals are required by OSHA to wear gloves for protection from the transfer-of-disease.

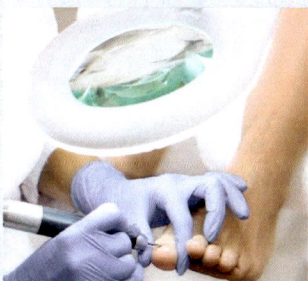

Gloves — or Not

It is important to note that while state boards do not mandate the wearing of gloves, OSHA regulations do for employee protection against the transfer of infections when there may be a danger of exposure.

What is the difference between two agencies? State boards are mandated to protect consumers (clients), while OSHA (Occupational Safety and Health Administration) is a federal agency mandated to protect all workers. The requirement for gloves by certain workers is required from OSHA to prevent the exposure to and the potential for transfer of disease from clients to workers.

States do mandate a cleanup policy in case of a blood spill, which includes even a tiny drop of blood. OSHA requires the prevention of exposure to it even before it happens. OSHA considers cleanup too late to protect the worker, though they do have rules for cleanup also.

Are nail professionals open to exposure to the transfer of disease? Are they ever exposed to even a single drop of blood? The answer is yes, they are. For that reason, OSHA requires nail professionals wear gloves and has since 2001. Further details can be found in the Appendix.

Analysis

The consistent performance of an analysis during a service establishes a standard of care. Although this practice is covered in nail training, it is often underemphasized, leading to its omission by many nail technicians in their actual services. Consequently, when a professional does perform this essential step, it stands out as a distinctive element of their service. This attention to detail not only differentiates the professional from others but also conveys to clients the importance of assessing the condition of their hands and feet to recommend the most suitable service. Clients may then question the absence of such care in other salons, leading to the realization that it signifies a higher level of concern for their well-being.

A good analysis is pivotal to providing a successful treatment to nail care clients.

The following describes the procedure for conducting an Analysis.

During a manicure, once clients have washed their hands and taken their seats, the professional begins the analysis immediately after the customary greeting. The Analysis proceeds as follows:

1. The professional instructs them to rest their hands on the table towel or mat, palms facing up.
2. The nail professional then gently takes each hand, one after the other, carefully examining the skin (flipping the hands to inspect the back) first and then the nails.
3. A pattern of analysis is developed by each professional. For the manicure, the hands are placed on the towel in front of the manicurist, palms up, and the process begin. For a pedicure, the professional assists in positioning each foot on the footrest, if not already placed, by supporting the ankle and the underside of the foot, guiding them onto the footrest. These preparatory positions set the stage for the commencement of the analysis.

It is essential to physically touch the skin during the analysis, and later the nails, to reinforce the client's perception that the nail professional is thoroughly examining their hands or feet for any signs of conditions. This tactile interaction serves as confirmation of the professional's attention to detail and care. The professional discusses the observed condition of the skin and, subsequently, the condition of the nails with the client.

Consultation

Following the analysis, the professional recommends a specific treatment and briefly touches upon home care. During the appointment, clients receive guidance on maintaining and enhancing the benefits of the service with home care products, fostering a collaborative approach to beauty care. The professional outlines the expected outcomes of a comprehensive treatment plan, advises on future appointments, and educates the clients on the significance of home care, including instructions on its execution and the recommended products.

Suggested Analysis/Consultation process

The Analysis and Consultation may appear seamless. Following describes the analysis/consultation, beginning when the nail professional takes each hand/foot.

1. *Determine the skin type and condition of the hands/feet*

2. *Ask questions to establish the probable causes for any conditions or problems*

3. *Suggest the appropriate service*

4. *Prescribe home care products and their use*

5. *Define and recommend possible changes in client activities*

6. *Outline a specific program for improving the look and condition of the hands/ arms and feet/legs, including homecare*

7. *Determine the condition of the nails*

8. *Recommend treatments for the nails*

9. *Begin the service.*

The transition between Analysis and Consultation is designed to be fluid. The process commences as the nail professional takes each hand or foot. The steps include identifying the skin type and condition, inquiring about potential causes for any observed issues, recommending suitable services, prescribing home care products along with usage instructions, suggesting modifications to the client's activities if necessary, and devising a tailored program to enhance the appearance and health of the hands/arms and feet/legs, which incorporates home care. Additionally, the condition of the nails is assessed, and treatments are advised before initiating the service.

Initially, the shift to skincare-based services may introduce a sense of awkwardness during analysis and consultation. To overcome this, professionals should engage in practice sessions, using colleagues or a significant other to simulate various conditions such as dry skin, nails, sunspots, and more. With practice, these assessments and conversations will become instinctive, allowing for swift and accurate identification of conditions.

Skin Structure Review:

For nail professionals to conduct precise analyses, a comprehensive understanding of skin structure is crucial. The skin, a protective and multifunctional organ, is composed of layers: the epidermis (outermost), the dermis (middle), and the subcutaneous (underlying support). The epidermis varies in thickness and is characterized by a continuous cycle of cell reproduction and shedding. This cycle culminates in the release of dead cells through desquamation.

The dermis, composed of dense fibrous connective tissue, is replete with circulatory and lymphatic vessels, along with nerve endings that traverse the subcutaneous layer. It consists of two distinct layers: the papillary, responsible for the ridged patterns that manifest as fingerprints, and the reticular, which is rich in collagen and elastin fibers that maintain skin's tone and flexibility. These fibers play a pivotal role in structural support and wound healing.

The subcutaneous layer, while not a component of the skin, serves as a bridge between the dermis and muscle tissue. It is populated with fat cells that function as a protective cushion and an energy reserve. The thickness of this layer is influenced by numerous factors, including age, sex, health, and body weight. Its functions extend to maintaining skin's smoothness, defining individual appearance, and supporting metabolic processes.

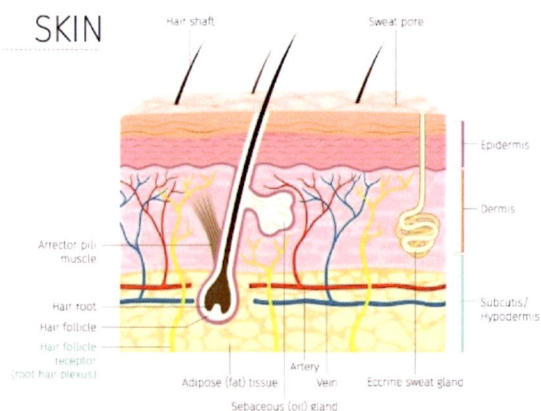

SKIN

Hair shaft · Sweat pore · Epidermis · Dermis · Arrector pili muscle · Hair root · Hair follicle · Hair follicle receptor (root hair plexus) · Subcutis/Hypodermis · Adipose (fat) tissue · Vein · Artery · Eccrine sweat gland · Sebaceous (oil) gland

Nail professionals who broaden their offerings to encompass skin treatments will focus on the epidermis. This layer reflects the skin's health, displaying softness and resilience when well-maintained and signs of distress otherwise. Professionals must evaluate the skin's requirements through careful analysis and propose suitable services through consultation, ensuring a delicate approach when discussing the skin's condition with clients.

Analysis of the skin

The first stage in tailoring treatments involves identifying the skin types and conditions of the hands and feet. Skin types denote the natural characteristics, whereas conditions are the outcomes of damage or environmental factors. These conditions can impact the skin's glands, hair, nails, and the tiny muscles responsible for goosebumps.

Analysis includes touching the skin

Facial skin types are classified as normal, dry, oily, combination, and sensitive, with the latter also potentially being a condition. Skin conditions encompass a range of issues like acne, sensitivity, aging, dehydration, rosacea, and more, including hyperpigmentation, eczema, psoriasis, and others. The skin types for hands and feet mirror those of the face, except for oily or acne-prone skin and rosacea. The subsequent list details the typical skin types found on hands and feet.

Analysis and Consultation

To perform appropriate care. the nail professional must possess a comprehensive understanding of skin types and conditions, as well as the client's overall health, existing conditions, and medications.

Treatments and home care necessitate that the nail professional possesses a comprehensive understanding of skin types and conditions, as well as the client's overall health, existing conditions, and medications.

Normal skin

This skin is characterized by its smooth, soft, and resilient nature, and requires preventive care to preserve its texture and moisture levels.

Treatment: The Hydrating Manicure or Pedicure is the suggested professional treatment.

Homecare: A weekly gentle scrub is recommended and the use of hydrating lotion and SPF protection to prevent hyperpigmentation.

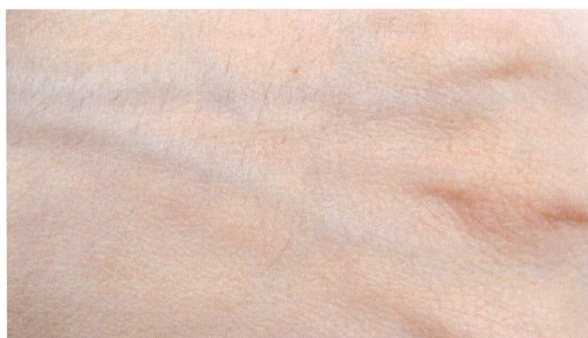

Normal skin is smooth and without wrinkles

Dry skin

This skin is parched-looking, with a lackluster appearance and noticeable wrinkles on the epidermis, often from external influences.

Treatment: This skin benefits from exfoliation and hydration-focused treatments. A gentle scrub is integral to the service to remove barriers to penetration of product ingredients during the treatment. Follow this with a hydrating mask with terry mitts, or, optionally, a paraffin treatment. Soaking should be avoided.

Homecare: This includes regular and intense hydration, sun protection, and bi-weekly gentle exfoliation.

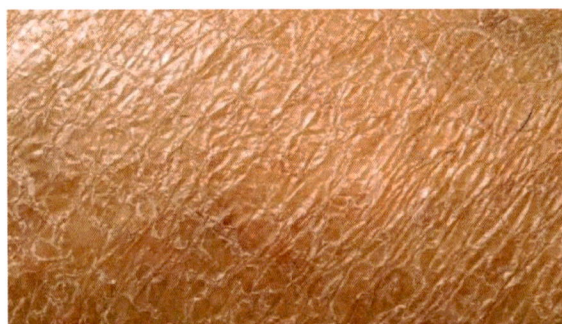

Dry skin may be rough and scaley.

Sensitive skin

Easily irritated and prone to adverse reactions, this skin requires a cautious approach.

Treatment: Start with a gentle introduction to products, testing for reactions, and progress to more intensive treatments if tolerated. Weekly manicures that build soon to a hydrating mask are advisable. Soaking and wet towels should be avoided, while hydration remains a priority.

Testing for Sensitivity
Testing for sensitivity is placing a dot of the hydrating mask on the inside of the forearm of the client as soon as sensitivity is verbally acknowledged. No masking is performed in this first appointment. If no sensitivity is noted after the first appointment, the second appointment can contain a short-time masking. If there is no response, normal protocol can be assumed in further appointments.

Conditions are present in all skin types and instill complexity in skin treatments, Listed below are those usually see on the hands and feet by nail professionals.

Homecare: Consistent use of lotion and sun protection that are fragrance free is important to healing.

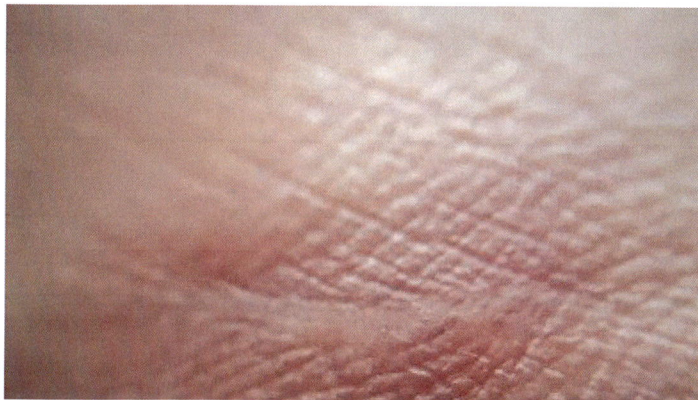

Sensitive skin can be red and red, blotchy and break out in hives or even lesions

Conditions are present in all skin types and instill complexity in skin treatments. Listed below are those usually seen on the hands and feet.

Dehydrated skin, characterized by fine lines and a thin, stressed appearance, requires a regimen focused on moisture replenishment. Start with a gentle exfoliation and rich hydration, gradually introducing more intensive treatments after the first appointment. Consistent hydration is vital, through a series of specialized manicures.

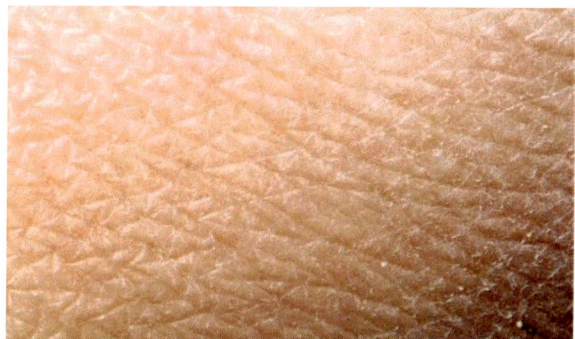

Dehydrated skin has fine lines and a stressed appearance.

31

Soaking should be avoided. Home care includes protective measures and regular application of hydrating products.

Treatment: It is essential to recognize that dryness is often due to internal influences. Begin with a light scrub to remove barriers to penetration during each visit. Follow this with hydrating masks, covering the treated area, and using low-heat mitts. The professional care aims to prepare the skin for the intense home care that this client must commit to performing.

A discussion concerning sufficient drinking of water is repeated several times during treatments, as well as the role of medications.

Homecare: Clients should identify the cause of their dehydration and take preventive or corrective measures. Intense use of hydrating lotion at bedtime is recommended, and in some cases, gloves may enhance the home treatment.

Calluses - Calluses on the hands and feet are common, varying in size from small to substantial. Although clients often request

> Blades and graters are dangerous and against the law for professional use in every state.

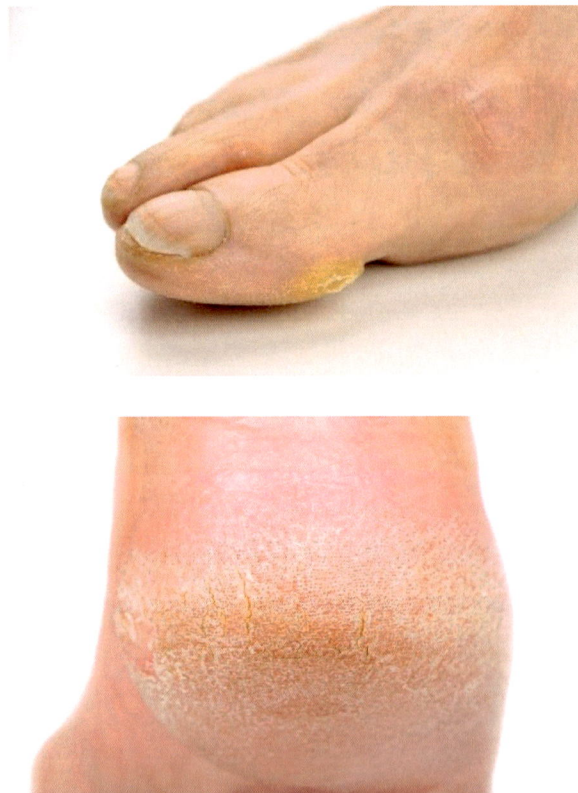

their removal, it is essential to reduce them rather than eliminate them entirely. Using a callus softening lotion facilitates this process.

Callouses occur on areas that are abraded by shoes or objects.

Treatment: Clients with heavy calluses benefit from a Callus Control Series, comprising of 6-8 weekly or bi-weekly visits. These treatments gradually reduce calluses, minimizing their likelihood of returning. For very thick calluses, weekly care is necessary until they become manageable. Understand that removing calluses with a blade leads to their speedy return, often harder and thicker, akin to scar tissue. Softening and gradual reduction are key. See the Appendix for the Protocol.

The professional treatment involves applying a callus softening product to the affected area, following the specified duration indicated in the product instructions. Next, abrasion of the callus occurs using an e-file or pedi-paddle, followed by hydrating lotion.

Pedi-Paddle vs. E-file

- Pedi-Paddle:
Flat and ideal for highly curved areas (e.g., edges of heels). However, it can inadvertently file skin outside the callus on flatter surfaces.

- E-file:
Precise placement for exfoliation when used by a well-trained professional.

Homecare: Recommend a scrub for home care, along with an AHA lotion applied nightly to the calluses. Light use of a pedi-paddle after showers twice weekly helps maintain results. Use hydrating lotion in the morning and after hand washing and apply SPF to the dorsum of the hands and feet in the morning. Note that AHA lotions may not suit everyone, and gradual introduction is advised, especially for those with sensitive skin. Discontinue use if redness occurs.

Mature – Considered both a skin type and a condition, mature skin can manifest across various skin types. Crêpey appearance (often due to dehydration) and varying degrees of wrinkles characterize mature hands and feet. Hyperpigmentation may also occur based on sun exposure over the years (see Hyperpigmentation).

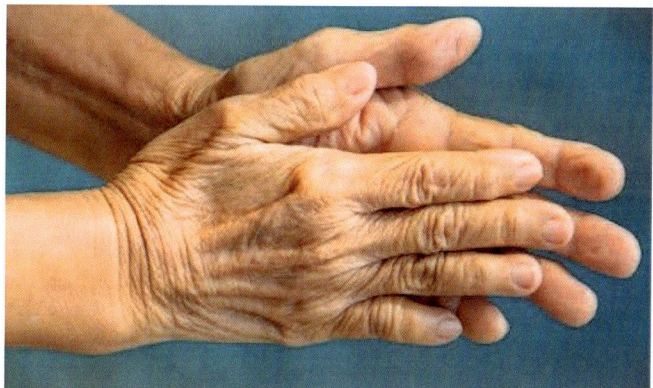

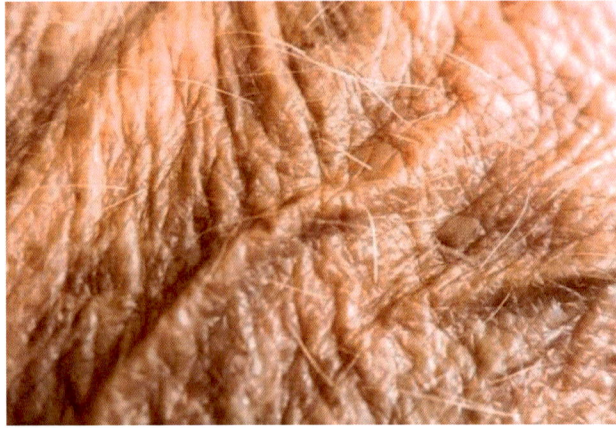

Mature skin is wrinkled and may also be dehydrated.

Treatment: Depending on the degree of aging, clients with mature skin may require an anti-aging series. Hydration is crucial in both professional treatments and home care. Incorporate a light treatment during the service (after the scrub).

Homecare: Encourage clients to protect their hands from moisture loss (e.g., wear gloves during chores). A consistent regimen of hydrating lotion and SPF after hand washing is essential. AHA lotions, while beneficial, require cautious use. Gradually introduce them, especially for those with sensitive skin, and discontinue if any adverse reactions occur.

For this client, nighttime use of a lotion containing an AHA ingredient is recommended. During the day, prioritize hydrating lotion and SPF. If AHAs are introduced, begin with alternate evening use for two weeks, closely monitoring for any reactions. Gradually increase to every evening, if well-tolerated. For ultra-sensitive individuals, opt for very low percentage lotions. AHA lotions contain in varying percentages (4% to 10%) for home care; choose lower percentages for sensitive clients. If the skin is sclerotic (hardened and dry), esthetic-level 20% AHA may be recommended for home care, with alternate evening for two weeks, and then, if tolerated, increase to every evening. SPF remains crucial.

Hyperpigmentation – Discoloration of the skin may be called "sunspots" or sun damage. Overexposure to the sun damages melanocytes in the basal layer of the epidermis, leading to dark spots during desquamation.

Treatment: Similar to mature skin care, incorporate skin brighteners. The term "lightener" is now replaced by "brighteners" due to the misconception that total lightening can be achieved. The term "skin bleaching" is now illegal for use as a treatment term in the US.

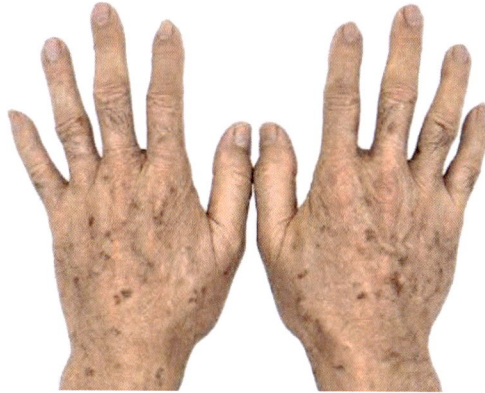

Environmentally exposed skin appears to have every condition, from dry to hyperpigmentation.

Homecare: Consistent use of skin brighteners is essential. These products may contain substitutes for hydroquinone, such as kojic acid, alpha arbutin, or azelaic acid. Combining brighteners with a low percentage of Retinol enhances their effectiveness. The home care recommended for mature skin is appropriate for this client.

Environmentally Exposed – These hands may exhibit various conditions due to overexposure to chemicals, water/solvents, sun, wind, weather, and abrasion. Callusing is common, especially on excessively barefoot feet or those in poorly fitting shoes. Hyperpigmentation typically appears around age forty.

Treatment: An anti-aging program with AHA and skin brighteners is recommended.

Homecare: Regular gentle scrubbing, nightly low percentage AHA lotion, hydrating SPF lotion in the morning and after hand washing, and anti-pigmentation lotions are essential.

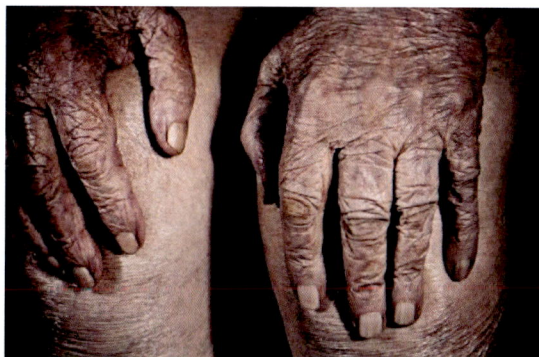

Environmentally exposed skin appears to have every condition, from dry to hyperpigmentation

Advanced knowledge of skin conditions and availability to effective home care products for these client conditions form the basis of successful treatment recommendations and support excellent results. Client commitment to home care is equally crucial for achieving optimal results.

Chapter 6

Nail Plate Analysis, Conditions, and Treatment

While skin type and conditions are initially noted, a comprehensive service also includes a detailed analysis of the client's nail plates, followed by consultation.

Analyzing the nail plates is an integral part of the overall service, not an afterthought. The professional finishes the skin analysis and then immediately transitions to the nail analysis. (Many professionals say, "OK, let's look at your nails now.") The movement appears seamless, with the overall analysis seen as one procedure.

Both skin and nail analyses are important to the recommendation of the treatment for the service and the home care advice.

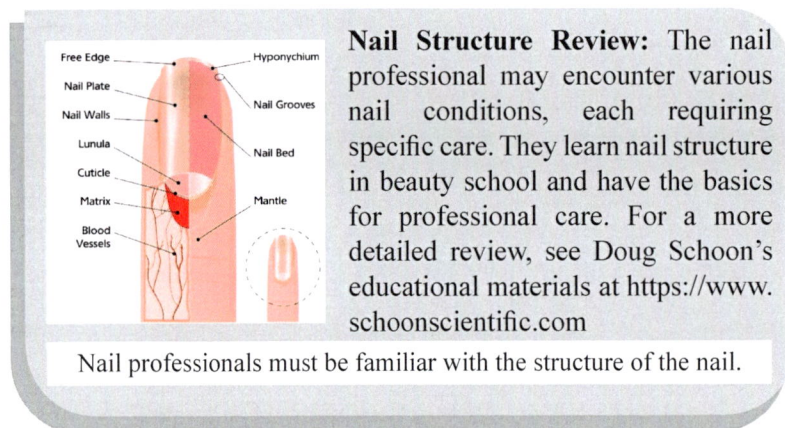

Nail Structure Review: The nail professional may encounter various nail conditions, each requiring specific care. They learn nail structure in beauty school and have the basics for professional care. For a more detailed review, see Doug Schoon's educational materials at https://www.schoonscientific.com

Nail professionals must be familiar with the structure of the nail.

Nail Conditions

Professionals may encounter various nail conditions, each requiring specific care. When the nail professional is analyzing the nail plates, one of seven most common conditions will be seen, each having its own causes and treatments. These conditions are:

Normal nails: They are strong but flexible with a shaped, opaque free edge. They resist breakage through their flexibility and have a uniform and healthy coloring on the nail bed and free edge. The service for these nails is maintenance, not resolution of a nail condition.

Treatment: The basic Soakless, Hydrating, or Aromatherapy services. It is the client's choice as per the professional's recommendation.

Home care: The client is recommended home care for the nail plates to maintain their health, flexibility, and strength. Picture Normal nails, no polish.

Peeling/Layering nails (Delamination): This problem will send a client to a nail professional faster than any other. Many of the nails, usually on the hands, may begin peeling/layering, but it may be only one due to chronic abuse. Frequent immersion in water, particularly with detergents, is known to cause layering by stripping natural oils and adhesives. The free edge peels apart, layer by layer, sometimes even into the area past the hyponychium, until they are thin and weak. They tear easily until there is no free edge.

Peeling or Layering can be an ongoing problem unless repaired and causative conditions are avoided.

Treatment: This person must have soakless manicures and pedicures as recommended by their nail professional. These nails will need a series of nail treatments weekly or bi-weekly until the nails strengthen to normal and/or the damaged nails grow off. This will take three to four months on the fingers, longer on a damaged great toe, though the matrix massage lessens this time. Periodic applications may be necessary for maintenance after successful treatment. Before and after photos are recommended to remind the client of the prior condition when they finally are healthy.

Unless this client is chronically ill and on detrimental medications, with commitment to professional and home care and removal of habits that cause the peeling, these nails can return to normal and be beautiful very quickly with committed professional and home care.

Before the development of effective treatments, many nail professionals brushed a thin layer of glue horizontally across the free edge of these nails before polishing as a deterrent to the peeling. The theory was that if you could keep them together until the layering area had grown out and been filed off, the nails would no longer layer. This theory may be true, but usually, this method is not effective as glue fatigues and ceases performing its adhesion duty with being immersed in water repeatedly and with the repeated bending of the weak nails.

Others believe a wrap is the answer, and this can work, though the wraps require weekly or bi-weekly maintenance on the thin and weak free edges for the same reason as the use of only glue. Other nail professionals will suggest enhancements to "cure" the problem by allowing the nails to grow past the peeling. This may or may not work, depending on the health of the client and the skill of the professional.

One treatment, the IBX System, has proven to be especially effective as a professional treatment for peeling natural nails. The product moves into the nail bed, repairing the damage so new healthy nail can grow in behind the damaged nail plate. The natural nail plate is reinforced and becomes immediately stronger and appears healthier.

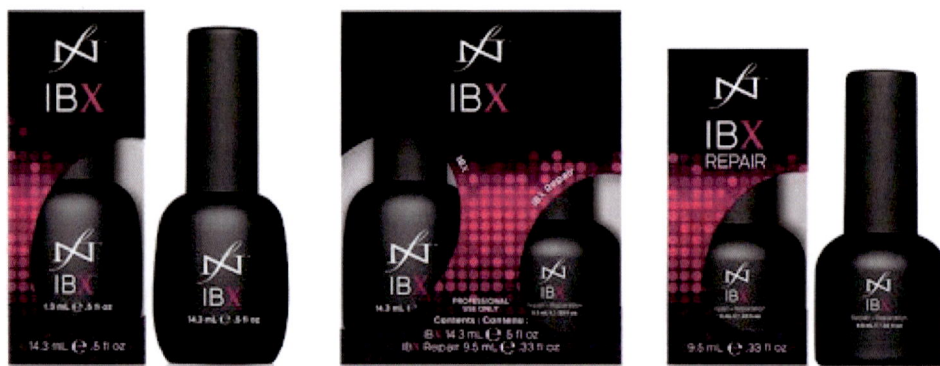

IBX from Famous Names is a proven excellent professional nail repair product

Home care: These nails need a home care treatment and massage every night with oils or nail repair products. Commitment to daily massage around and on the nail, and especially on the matrix, is important to enhance and maintain the strength and flexibility of the nail plates. Massage of the area enhances the penetration of the ingredients while also increasing circulation to the matrix for the development of a healthier nail plate.

The client must understand that no treatment "cures" future peeling unless the causes of the condition are eliminated. Recommendations by the nail professional for treatments and home care are especially important for this client.

Vertical Splitting nails: These nails begin to split usually due to damage in the matrix, but aging and dryness also can cause the splitting. It begins at the free edge and proceeds to split back to the hyponychium, occasionally beyond if forced apart. Even short nails split for this person. Some splits may be permanent and require continual management.

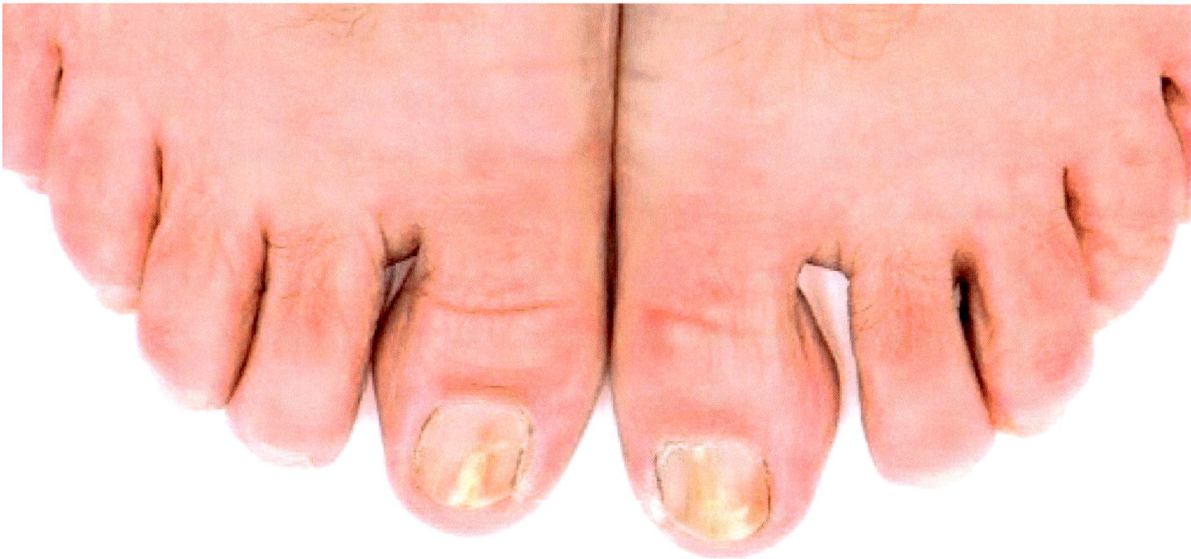

Vertical splits, onychorrhexis, is a split from the free edge towards the base of the nail. This can be a forever problem but can be repaired to reduce the frustration of tearing clothing, etc.

Treatment: Glue the split together and then apply a repair wrap or builder gel nail over it to hold it together. Wraps last between appointments if the client wears gloves but usually need reapplication every two weeks to a month. Gels/gel polish can be worn over it and will protect the wrap from water damage to extend their wear. Enhancements of any type can be included in the treatment, with the required maintenance until the nail has fully grown out unless it is a permanent split.

Clients with permanently split nails appreciate this repair and become loyal clients. They learn quickly after the damage is apparent that if they do not deal with it on an ongoing basis, they must trim the nail back to the hyponychium often or it catches on everything. If the damage is due to damage to the matrix, it permanently splits and needs repair continual repair, or the tearing of clothing becomes very annoying to client.

Home care: The client must be told to wear protective gloves while working in water or the wrap releases very soon. Also, immersion in water makes the splitting happen faster. If the damage is not to the matrix and is dryness and/or damage, matrix massage with an excellent product daily can prevent this condition.

Brittle nails: This free edge breaks with little pressure due to brittleness. There is no crack in the nail; it just comes off in a chunk. Clients usually refer to the break as making a snapping sound.

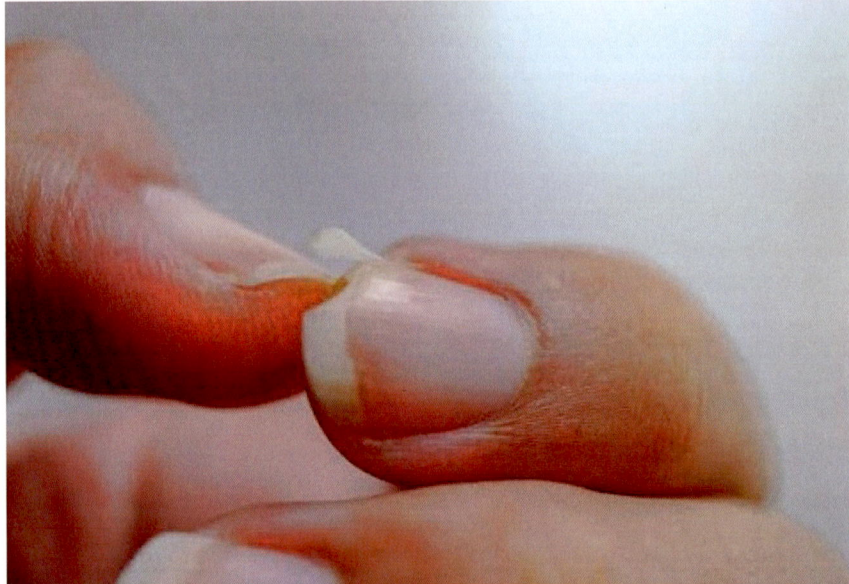

Brittle nails are aggravating to sufferers. One minute they have a nice nail, the next it is gone, with a snap.

Treatment: The manicures for these nail conditions are good hydrating treatments best performed in a structured series. A hydration treatment is imperative to improvement, plus the recommendation of and encouragement of the client in performing home care.

Home care: This nail is brittle and dry due to the client being in poor health, heredity, or exposure to water often. Treatment at home between appointments with an effective treatment product and massage is imperative. Massaging the product on the nail twice daily, and on the sidewalls and matrix area, brings flexibility to the nails, and a healthier, more flexible nail is produced.

Committed treatment with oils or WellNail achieves and maintains a healthy appearance and flexibility. These treatments, even over polish, can improve the condition of the nails through improvement of the matrix health and product "creep" under the nail bed from the sidewalls.

Eggshell nails: These nails, called hapalonychia nails, are thin and weak and peel off with little effort or accidental pressure. This condition is usually on all the nails on the hands, never just one nail. Many times, they appear to grow down over the end of the finger, adhering closely to the skin at the tip of the finger. Malnutrition, illness, and medications can contribute to this condition.

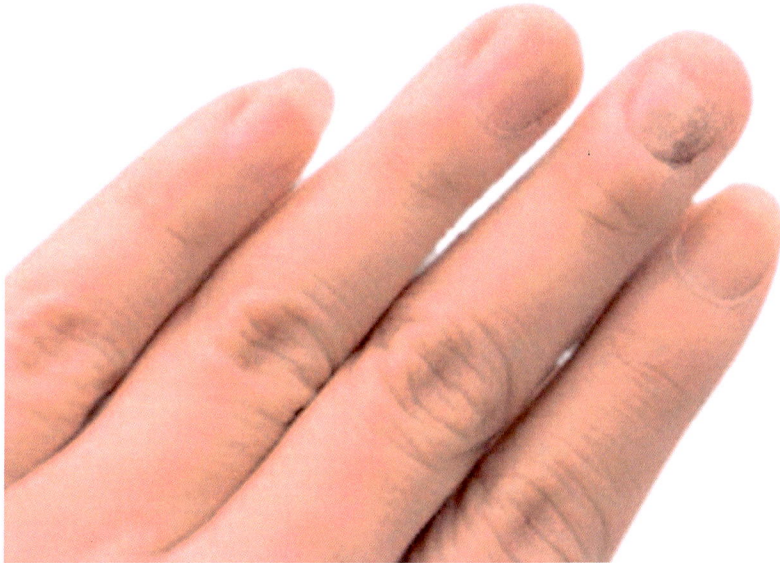

Eggshell and lacy nails are so weak they split with the slightest touch.

Treatment: The IBX System series is highly effective on this condition. Clients with eggshell nails who want beautiful natural nails can have them with this treatment and good home care, including matrix massage. Many professionals suggest enhancements, such as gels, acrylics, or a repair wrap as it covers the problem and the client has beautiful nails, but it does not change the condition of the nail plate.

Home care: The nails must have nightly massage with a moisturizing or hydrating treatment product, such as WellNail. It is especially important to increase the health of the new, growing nail plate.

Lacy nails: These are eggshell nails, but the free edge seems thinner than even eggshell. Some areas of the free edge will appear translucent while others will be opaque, causing a lace-like appearance. They snag and tear clothing and hosiery so these clients seldom can grow a free edge to any significant length. They become very frustrated with their nails and are very appreciative when a nail professional can "fix" them. And they become a regular client!

Treatment: Nail plate treatment is indicated for professional care in a series, but also a treatment with a matrix/nail massage over a treatment oil or WellNail should be performed by the nail professional to ensure the client knows how to perform it at home.

Home care: Until the damaged nail is grown off, twice-daily treatment massage produces obvious results when teamed with IBX. Then, after the damage grows off, nightly matrix/nail massage is important to maintain for keeping them healthy and strong though flexible nails. It works, with compliance, and the nail professional must get that agreement from the client!

Ridges: Vertical ridges may appear suddenly on one or all nail plates. If it is on a single nail plate, it can usually be attributed to trauma of the matrix, while having them on most or all nails can be attributed to aging, a medical condition, and occasionally systemic dryness.

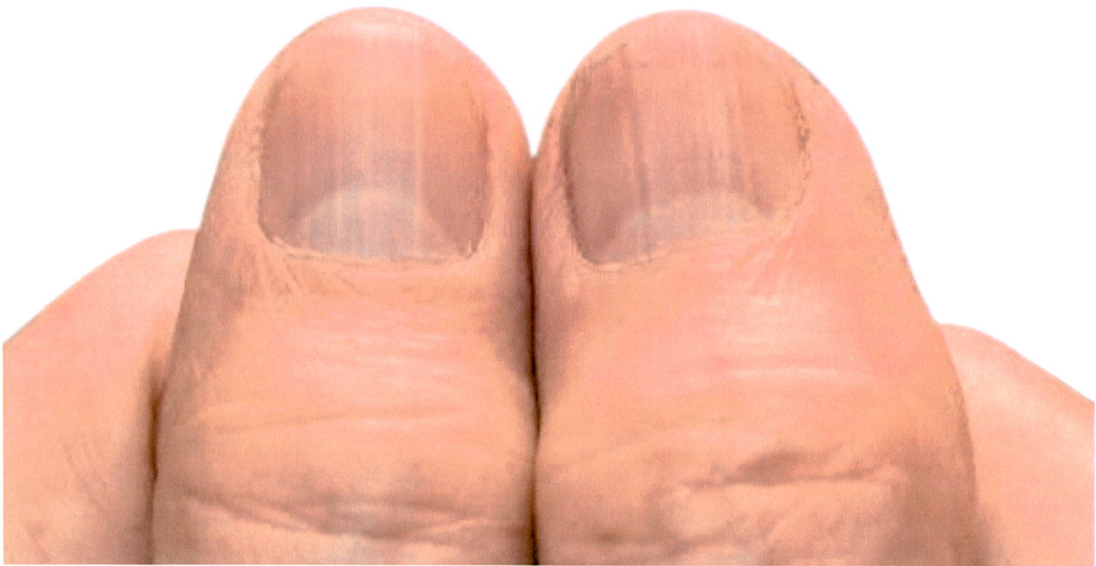

Ridged nails present on all nails indicates they are caused by aging, genetics, or dryness.

Treatment: Do not buff away the ridges as that thins the nail plate, though some can be done. Instead, use ridge filler under the polish. A nail plate treatment can improve the growing out nail plate, such as IBX, but the nail will have to grow out completely for the ridges to be gone or improved, and then homecare must continue.

Home care: Matrix massage with a treatment oil or WellNail can reduce the ridges dramatically as the nail grows out, especially if they are caused by aging or dryness.

Stress breaks: These nails give the impression of being too strong. They appear thick and healthy, then suddenly there is a crack on the side at the stress area. The stress point is where the hyponychium meets the free edge at the side fold, straight across to the other side, and is where the nail usually bends when hit directly on the end of the free edge. These nails may have had long-term overexposure to a form of formaldehyde in nail hardeners, which is recommended by some professionals for weak nails, or it may be a hereditary trait to have hard nails. Also, some clients believe constant tapping of the end of the free edge, such as on computer boards, can stimulate the growth and thickness/hardness of these nails if they already tend to be too stiff.

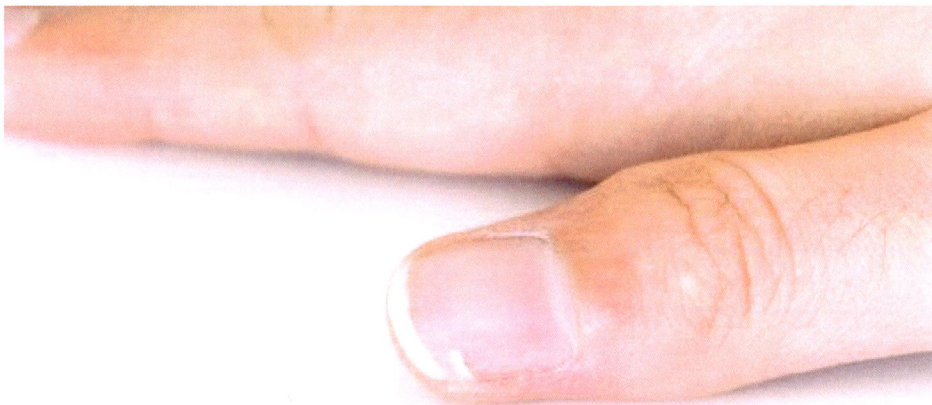

Stress breaks indicate the nails are inflexible, too hard, so they break at the stress point of the nail plate.

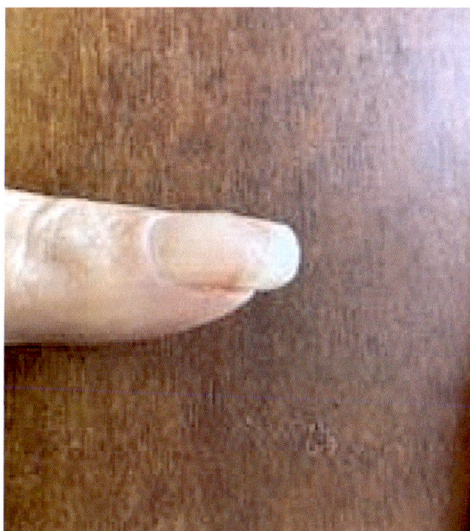

This nail is broken horizontally at the stress point.

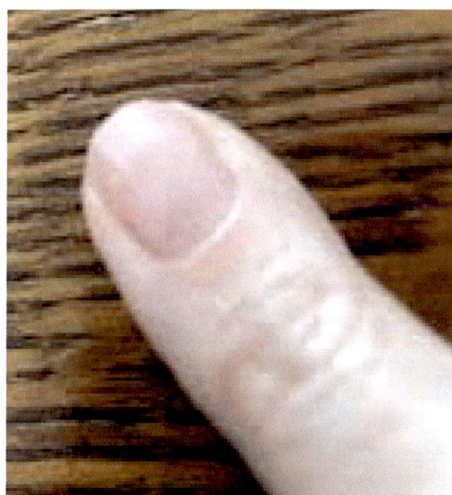

Without a repair, the nails breaks off within a day or two.

Treatment: Glue the break in the nail and allow to dry. Then a nail repair is essential, or it is gone within days, and it may be a painful tear behind the hyponychium. Apply a layer of glue vertically over the break, then a layer of fiberglass wrap mesh goes over the entire break vertically. Apply more glue and then a layer of fiberglass mesh wrap is laid horizontally across the stress point and the break. Glue again. Allow to fully dry or spray with an accelerator. Smooth the edges to make it invisible and apply polish or gel polish. This will need to be removed and reapplied bi-weekly with acetone until it is grown out or is long enough to shorten the nail to past the break. These nails tend to grow quickly, however, so one application may be sufficient.

Home care: These nails need a good oil or WellNail massaged on the matrix and surrounding tissues every night, forever, post wrap. Massaging over the matrix, nail plate, and sidewalls with treatments increases flexibility on the growing out nail plate and prevents breakage except under extreme conditions. The current nail plate will be more flexible, but the new growth nail plate will be even more healthy and flexible.

Nail biter nails (Onychophagy): These nails are bitten by the bearer and can be bitten far past the hyponychium in a severe case. They come to a nail professional in hopes they can break their habit. Professionals can often assist in breaking the habit, though success varies.

Treatment: Two choices are available, one being the performance of weekly manicures to encourage breaking the habit, the other being the application of enhancements. Both are accompanied by activities to break the habit.

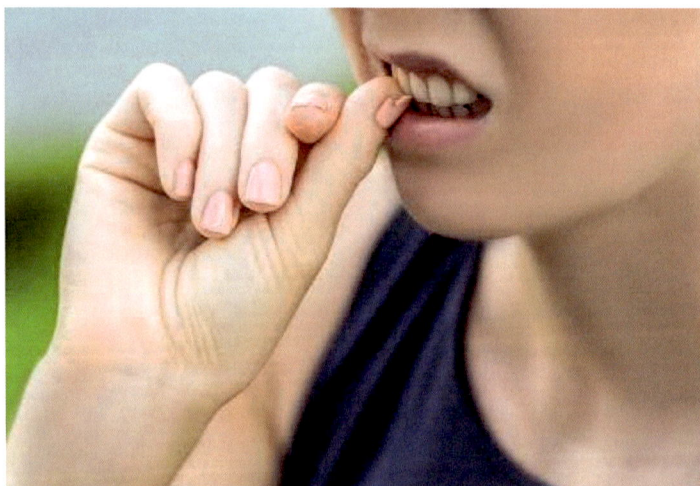

Nail biters want to quit biting and nail professionals can help them break the habit.

Home care: The client is recommended intense hydration around the nails and on the matrix, as with oils or WellNail every night and anytime the urge to bite is present.

After Enhancement nails: These nails are thin and weak, though they will vary in health according to

1) the skill and care of the technician,

2) the health of the client's nails,

3) the general health of the client, and

4) the technique of the removal.

Over prepping by the technician in the application area causes thin nails post enhancements. Incorrect and/or overuse of an e-file during prep and finish of the enhancements will also cause severe trauma. One example can be seen as markings in the nail plate, "rings of fire," curved ditches in the nail which are burns by the e-file into the nails as the artificial nails are finished.

Correct application of products and finish will not produce an unhealthy nail, though it may be more flexible for a brief time after removal of the enhancement product due to retained hydration from the coverage by the enhancement.

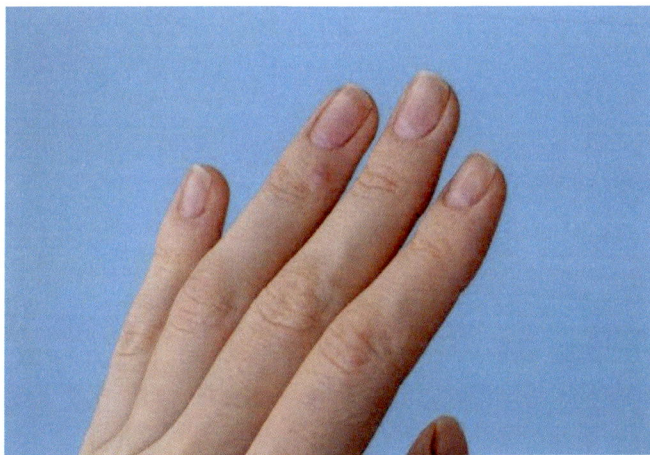

After Enhancement Nails vary in condition according to the skill of the nail artist.

Treatment: Nail treatment manicures are recommended after removal to support the newly exposed nail plate, producing obvious results and strength of the nail plate immediately. It is advised that clients come in for weekly care until the hydration is reduced and the nail is strong and growing.

Home care: Applying a treatment oil or WellNail to the nail and the skin surrounding the nail nightly, including massage of the matrix, is essential. The client must wear gloves when working with water to protect the nails.

Yellow nails: Nail technicians rarely see these nails, but when they do, the client must be questioned about the cause. Is it staining from a particular use? Did it suddenly appear? If there appears to be no targeted reason, the client should be referred to a dermatologist to investigate the cause. Potential causes are smoking, underlying health conditions such as diabetes, thyroid disorder and rheumatoid arthritis, trauma, fungal infection, nail polish staining, circulation issues, and buildup of lymphatic fluid around the lungs. Whether it is a single nail, or all nails is important.

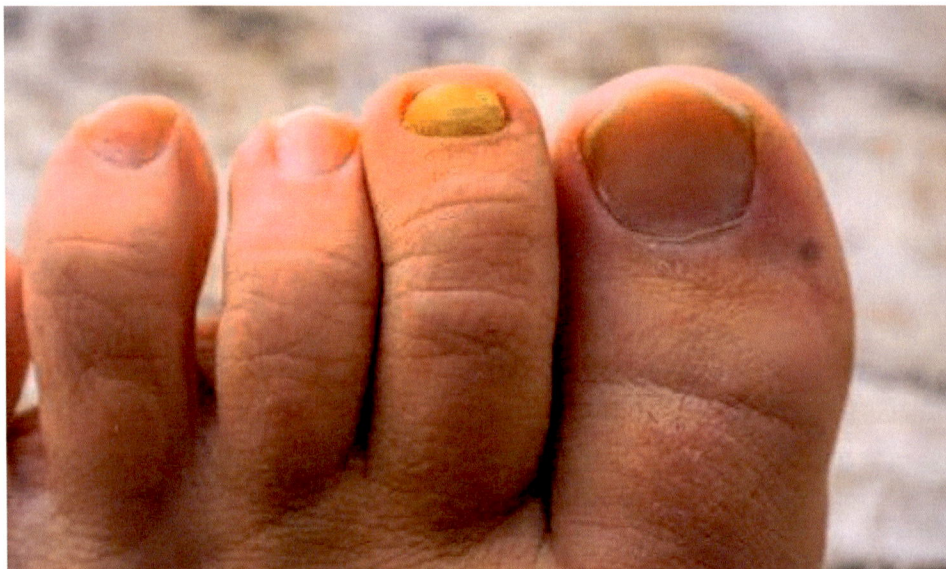

If discoloration of the nail plates is obvious, the client needs to investigate what the cause is to ensure it is not caused by an illness. Refer the client to a dermatologist.

Treatment: Always use a base coat, and refrain from allowing staining of the nails by outside activities, such as smoking. Apply a clear coat of base and topcoat over nails if no color is desired.

Home care: Always use a good basecoat when polishing nails, and always wear a protective basecoat and topcoat when not wearing color.

Discolored nails: This can happen for many reasons, including medications, no use of base coat or use of a poor basecoat under deeply pigmented polish, smoking when no polish is present, even tanning sprays on bare nails.

Cancer Treatment Nails: Chemotherapy can cause damage to the nails from within. Manicures can delay undesirable effects and provide the support the sufferer needs to manage nail conditions. Many chemo patients also say the home care is calming and relaxing. The emotional support of having beautiful nails during this time is invaluable.

Most seen conditions on nails during cancer treatment include:

- Inflammation and swelling

- Onycholysis – lifting of the nails from the nail bed, one or more to all nails

- Ridges – on the same nails on each hand or all nails

- Breaking and splitting nails – dehydrated, damaged from within

- Changes in pigmentation (e.g., hyperpigmentation, staining) may or may not be permanent

- Bacterial/Fungal infections – due to lower immune resistance

- Thickened or thinning nails – a response according to treatment care

- Leukonychia – tiny, white spots growing out from the back reflecting treatment, usually temporary

- Subungual hemorrhage – splinter or spot; trauma of the treatments

- Rarely, loss of all nail plates due to internal damage; they usually grow back after the cancer treatments cease but may be misshapen

Treatment: The nails of a person going through cancer treatments will reflect the overall health of the person and the invasiveness of the treatments. Weekly manicures will help, as will nail plate and skin care treatments. A discussion with the cancer treatment team is recommended to ensure treatments are permissible.

Home care: Massage of the matrix, surrounding skin, and nail plate nightly with a nourishing treatment is important. Any enhancement should be cleared by their cancer treatment team.

Cancer of the Nails

Cancer of the nails is rare but can be deadly if not detected early. Nail Professionals must be educated in its appearance and potentials to refer clients to medical care. On the nails, the darkness begin usually under the eponychium or at the nail fold and proceeds into the nail. The color is dark, but not caused by bruising.

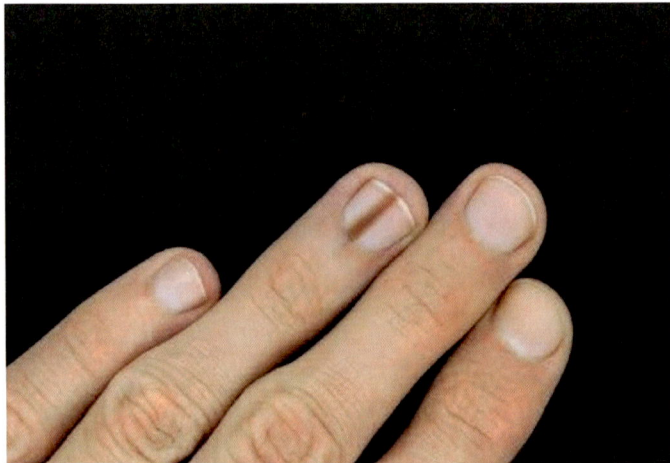

Melanoma of the nail many times is mistaken for trauma. Any client with a "bruise" that 1) they do not remember trauma to cause it and 2) it does not begin to grow off should be sent immediately to a physician for biopsy.

Melanoma of the Nails: Melanoma of the nail many times is mistaken for trauma. Any client with a "bruise" that:

1. the client does not remember the trauma to cause it
2. does not begin to grow off noticeably before the next appointment in a month
3. has darkened further, client should be sent immediately to a physician.

This cancer is treatable if diagnosed early and properly. If not, it will metastasize and can be deadly. Nail professionals have saved many lives through referrals in these cases.

Cancer of the Skin

Cancer on the skin (melanoma) on the feet is not usually found early as most people do not check the bottoms of their feet and believe those on the top or toes are bruises. This usual late diagnosis leads to this being a very high rate of morbidity in this cancer.

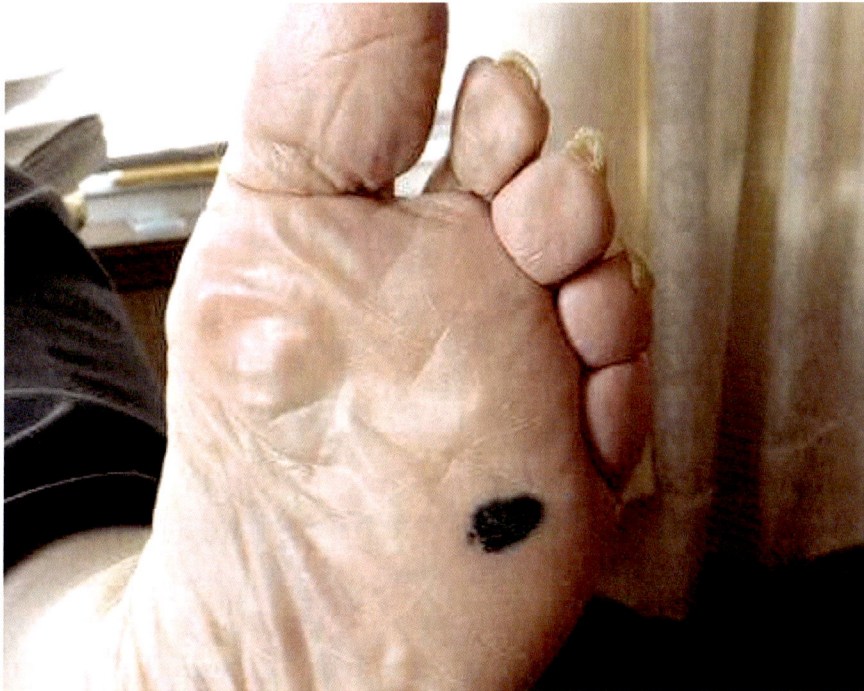

Melanoma on the plantar surface of the feet may go unnoticed as most people do not check the bottom of the feet.

This case was accidentally found when a patient was on the table being checked for another illness. The nurse walked past his bare feet and just happened to notice the lesion. It was treated, but had metastasized into the liver and the patient died of liver cancer. Melanoma metastasizes quickly through the lymphatic system so early treatment is important.

Nail professionals must check the hands and feet at every service for potentials of melanoma lesions. No resolution between one service and the next of symptoms indicates a need for a referral to a dermatologist (hands) or podiatrist (feet).

Before and after pictures are important for treating all these clients. (Remember the waiver.) Home care products are also important to these conditions, and instruction in the home care must be taught to the clients in a partnership mode, meaning the professional is a guide and performs the professional care to initiate and keep the improvement going, but the client is responsible for maintaining the improvement between treatments.

Natural nail professionals are presented with these nail conditions and must become comfortable with recommending and performing the care. Transforming a client from poor to excellent condition is very satisfying to a specialist, but it requires commitment on the part of both the professional and the client to achieve client goals. The desired goal is never achieved in one manicure or pedicure, and this must be explained to clients prior to treatment care.

Chapter 7

Analysis of the Skin and Nails on the Feet

Manicures and pedicures are different, though not in the basic protocols. Their difference lies in their analysis, in what the professional observes, and in the feet being an even more serious reflection of the overall health of the client. Yes, fingernails do reflect the health of the client, but the feet much more so due to their position at the "end of the line" in the body's circulatory system, and in how circulation in the feet is affected by various illnesses. Footwear also impacts the feet, either positively or negatively.

The conditions of the hands and feet, arms and their nails may reflect the overall health of the client.

A Story: At the Pool on Vacation

Denise Baich, The Pedicure Plus, St. Louis, MO, and her husband were relaxing by a pool at a resort in the Bahamas. Her husband, who had been attentive since she beacame an ANT and MNT many years before, leaned over and said, "Denise, look at the bottom of that guy's foot across the pool." She did and noticed an obvious "discoloration" on the bottom of his foot. It was clear to them that it was not from walking around the pool. Later, her husband urged, "You need to talk to him. You will never forgive yourself if you don't." So, she approached the man with a business card, apologized for the intrusion, and explained her profession. She then pointed out what she had observed and asked if she could take a picture of it with his phone to show him. She did, and he was shocked! He had never inspected his feet and was unaware of the discoloration. He mentioned that he regularly visited his dermatologist every three months and had an upcoming appointment. He promised to show the dermatologist the large, darkened area on his foot. (He noted that the dermatologist never examined his feet!) He was grateful and said he would inform her of the dermatologist's findings. This incident was recent, and he had not yet contacted her before the publication of this book. Regrettably, she did not capture the image on her own phone.

Chronic illnesses affect the feet, so the feet often reflect the presence of illness, sometimes even before the client is aware of the illness. Pedicure specialists trained in recognizing signs of illness on the feet can shorten or alleviate the suffering of these clients, and even save lives by strongly suggesting they consult their physician or podiatrist immediately. This is particularly true when these professionals are properly trained in analysis and have a referral system established with a physician/podiatrist.

Physicians and nail professionals can have a synergistic relationship that will grow the clientele of each at a much faster rate than if they did not collaborate. Dr. Steven Frank, DPM, and Denise Baich, MNT, have had a referral relationship for seven years and is still ongoing. They grew each other's businesses along the way.

Those who wish to specialize in pedicures have a responsibility to educate themselves about what they might observe on the feet of their clients and when to refer them to a podiatrist or physician. Clients can be directed to their own physician or podiatrist, or to one with whom the nail professional has established a relationship. A collaboration should be formed with trusted physicians and podiatrists for referrals. Trust must be mutual for a successful partnership.

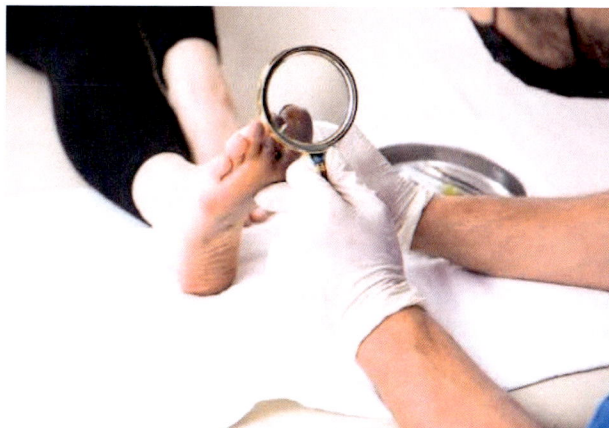

The Analysis step in pedicures is especially important due to the feet being an important mirror of illness in the body.

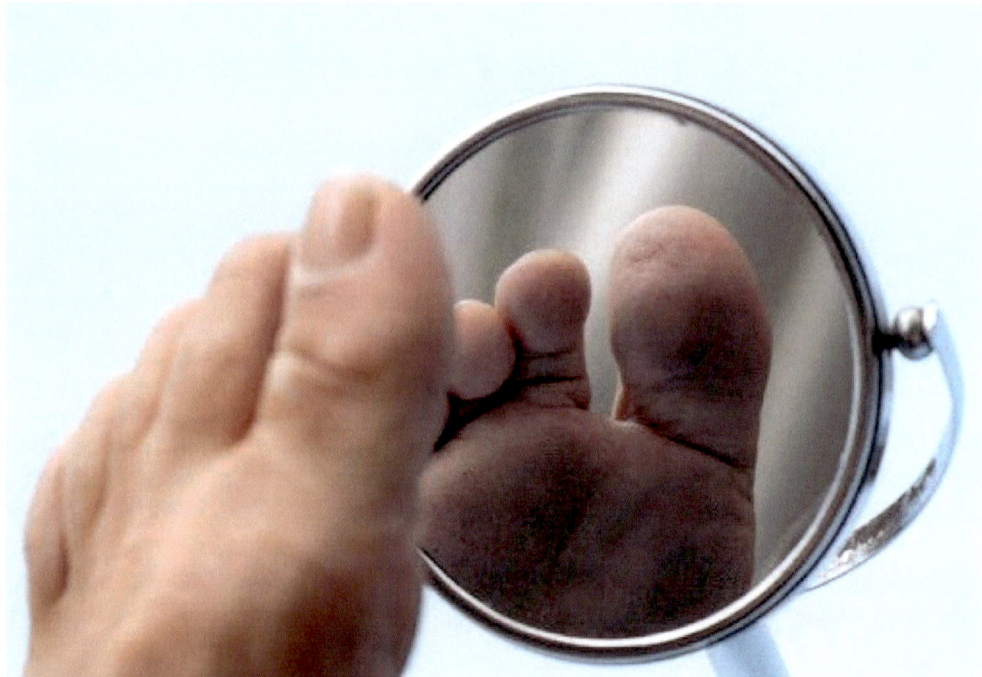

Training clients to check the bottom of their feet can save their life.

Conditions of the Feet: Below is a list of conditions pedicurists may encounter in clients, which they need to recognize. These conditions are not treatable by pedicurists but are listed here to inform them of precautions in their care and to know when to refer clients to a physician.

This list includes the most seen illnesses noted on New Client Sheets and on the feet by pedicurists; it is not exhaustive. Professionals who wish to work with chronically ill clients should undertake comprehensive courses designed to provide information for that specialty, such as those offered at www.nailcareacademy.com. A partial list is below.

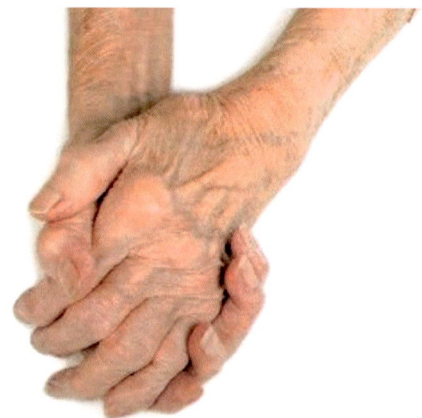

Arthritis is reflected in the feet and hands of the sufferer and their nail professional must focus on gentle care during their pedicures and to referring them to their physician if changes warrant an appointment.

Arthritis: Arthritis causes swelling and tenderness in one or more joints. Types of arthritis include osteoarthritis, psoriatic arthritis, and rheumatoid arthritis. It can affect individuals of any age, gender, or ethnicity, but is most found in women. Precautions during massage include avoiding pressure on joints and refraining from pulling on any joint.

Edema/Pitted Edema: Edema refers to swelling caused by fluid leakage into tissues and retained. Lymphedema, a form of edema, results from lymph vessel blockage. Peripheral edema primarily affects the arms and legs. Pitted edema occurs when pressing on an edematous area leaves an indentation. Traditional massage is contraindicated for edema or lymphatic edema. Avoid cuts or punctures, as healing is slow, and infections can occur.

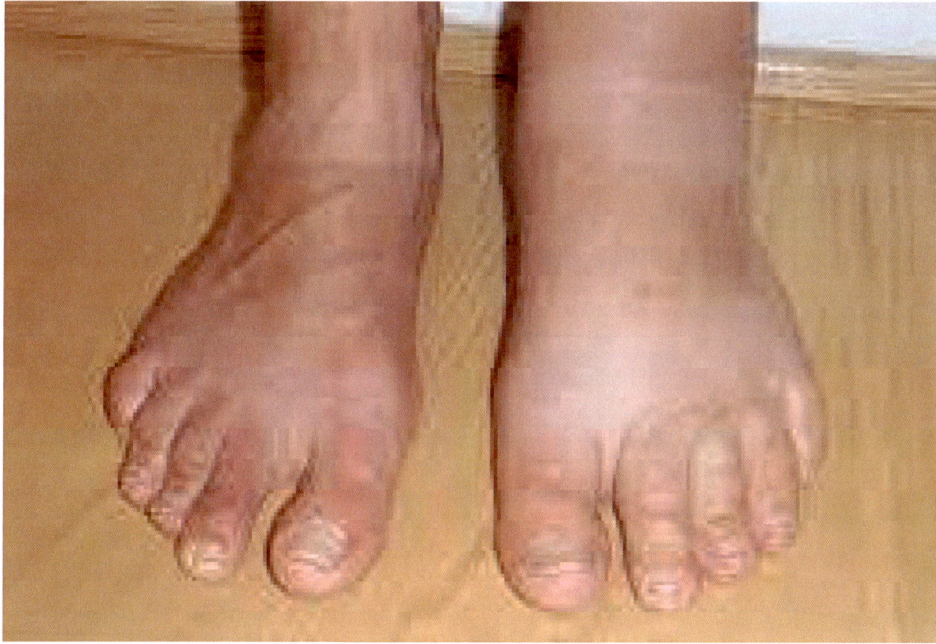

Edema is a circulatory condition, work carefully on these clients. No soaking is allowed.

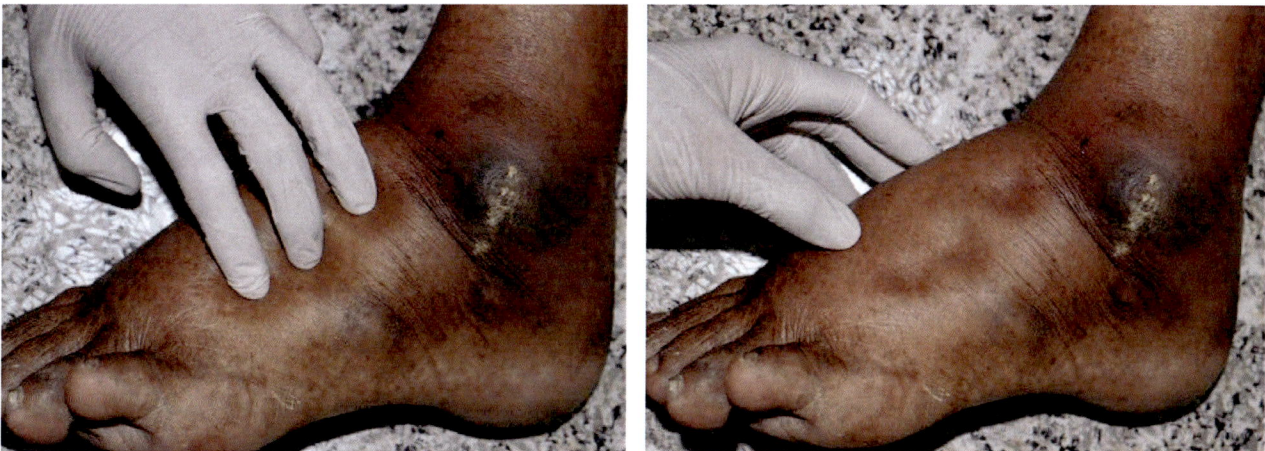

Pitting edema is a diagnostic tool and condition of edema. The fingers are pressed into the appendage and then lifter. The pits are still indented far longer than a healthy foot.

Neuropathy: Peripheral neuropathy damages nerves outside the brain and spinal cord, often associated with conditions like diabetes. It leads to numbness and pain, described as stabbing, burning, or tingling, especially in the hands and feet. Nail professionals may notice signs of neuropathy in clients on the feet, even if they appear normal.

This numbness can lead to undetected injuries which may lead to severe infections and amputations. Nail professionals must check for injuries at every service.

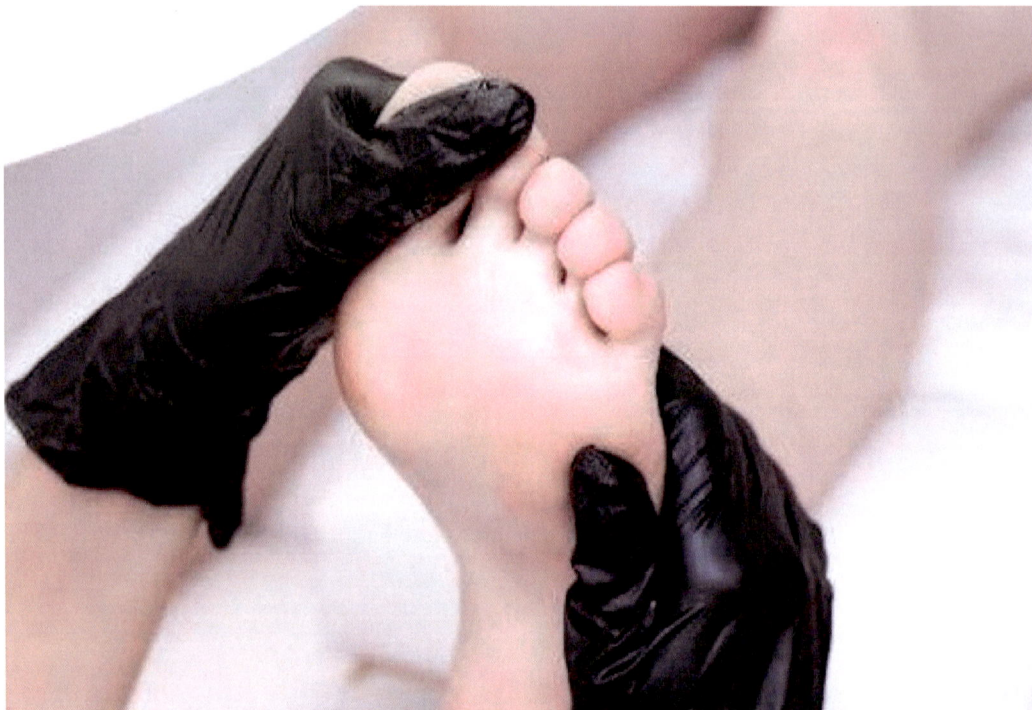

Nail professionals should check for neuropathy on diabetics and others. The analysis on these clients must be very thorough as they many times do not know they have injured themselves.

Diabetic Ulcers: An open wounds that take more than two weeks to heal despite treatment are considered chronic wounds. Diabetic ulcers are usually on the lower leg, ankle or foot as a result of poor circulation, and many become chronic due to their difficulty to treat.

Treatment: Any open wound is immediately referred to a physician.

PAD (Peripheral Artery Disease): PAD results from narrowed arteries (atherosclerosis), reducing blood flow to the head, arms, stomach, legs, and feet. Leg pain during walking is a common symptoms. Obtain permission from the client's physician for massage, and avoid deep muscle techniques. Gentle tapotement can be used for short durations. No service should be performed on a client with an open ulcer, but foot-only services, such as trimmings, are possible if no ulcers are present on the foot. These clients cannot be soaked.

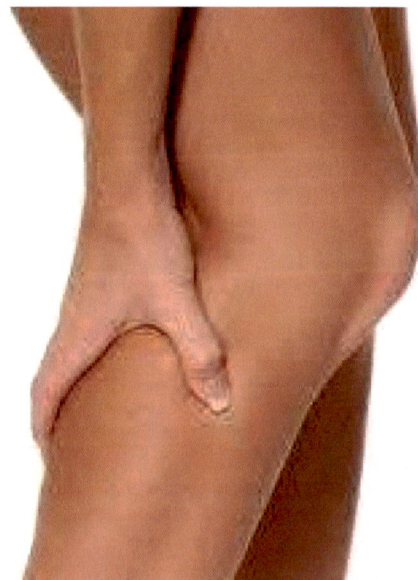

PVD (Peripheral Venous Disease): PVD ulcers (90% of cases) are typically found on the inside of the leg, just above the ankle, and on the heels, feet, and toes. Tight or itchy skin may precede them, and they heal slowly. Obtain permission from the client's physician for massage with a history of PVD, using gentle tapotement. Avoid service if an ulcer is open, but foot-only services are permissible if no ulcers are present on the foot.

Pre-Ulcers: Pre-ulcers are the initial stage of an ulcer, not yet broken through the skin. In Caucasians, the skin appears reddened; in individuals with skin of color, it may appear darker, blue, or purple. Pre-ulcers feel warmer, sore to the touch, and firmer than surrounding skin. They may itch. If a noticeable border exists beneath the skin, the ulcer is soon to be visible. Urgently refer clients to a physician for diagnosis and care without attempting to diagnose or speculate on the condition.

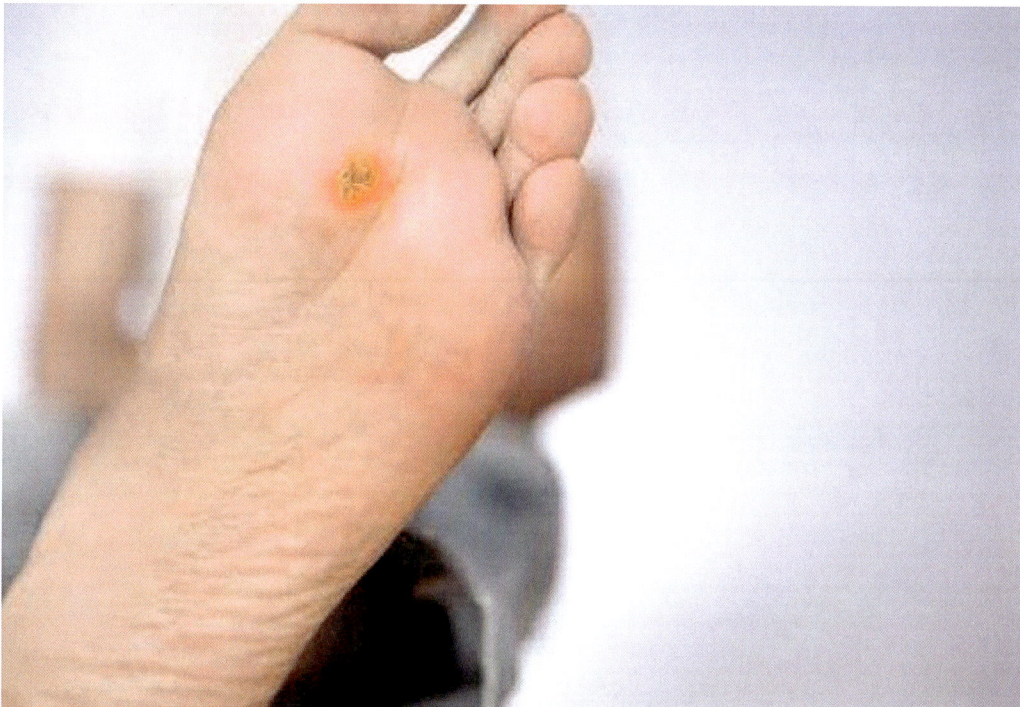

Pre-Ulcers are vague and may not be what they appear to be. Check for a bordered slight discoloration for a suspect area that may be a coming ulcer. Do not diagnose, but suggest the client see a podiatrist or diabetic specialist soon.

Nail professionals can detect pre-ulcers through touch if they pay close attention during an analysis. When an area is noted, the professional should draw the client's attention to it and refer them to their physician immediately, as early detection significantly reduces their suffering.

Clients with a history of Diabetes Mellitus, PAD or PVD require thorough evaluation before any service and should never experience traditional massage.

Eczema: Eczema presents as itchy patches on the hands, elbows, and other body areas. Although incurable, it is episodic, with triggers often related to stress and anxiety. Nail professionals should avoid performing services on irritated skin.

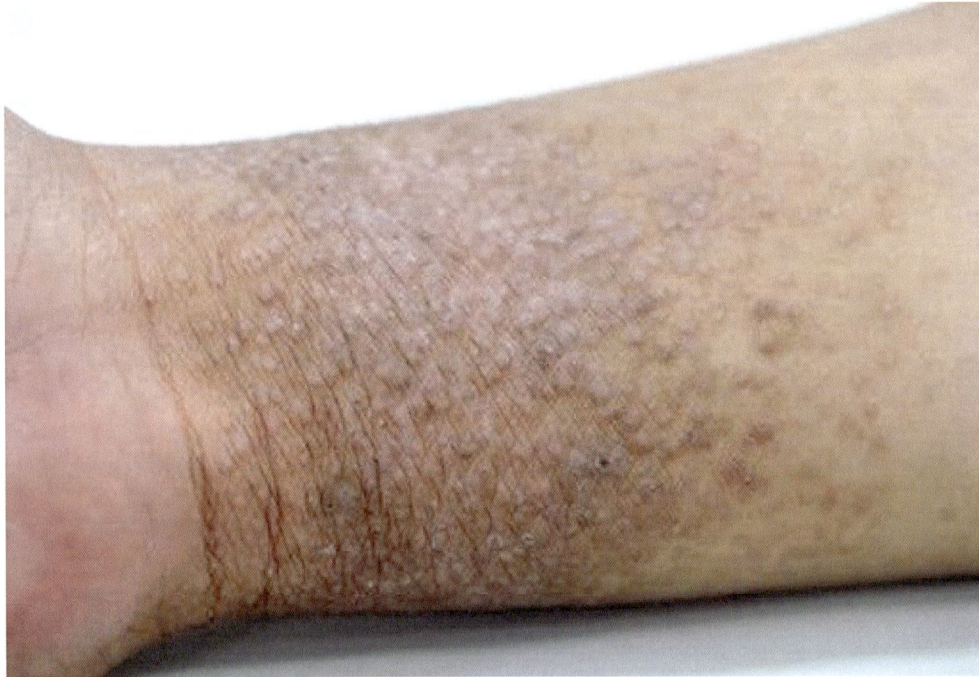

Eczema patients are accustomed to their having to constantly monitor skin for episodic occurrences of the condition. Few will come in for care during an episode, but a nail professional must be familiar with it.

Psoriasis: Psoriasis is another episodic condition that can be quite restricting to clients. Psoriasis is a skin disease that causes a rash with itchy, scaly patches, most commonly on the knees, elbows, trunk and scalp.

According to Mayo Clinic, psoriasis is a common, long-term (chronic) disease with no cure. It can be painful, interfere with sleep and make it hard to concentrate. The condition tends to go through cycles, flaring for a few weeks or months, then subsiding for a while. Common triggers in people with a genetic predisposition to psoriasis include infections, cuts or burns, and certain medications.

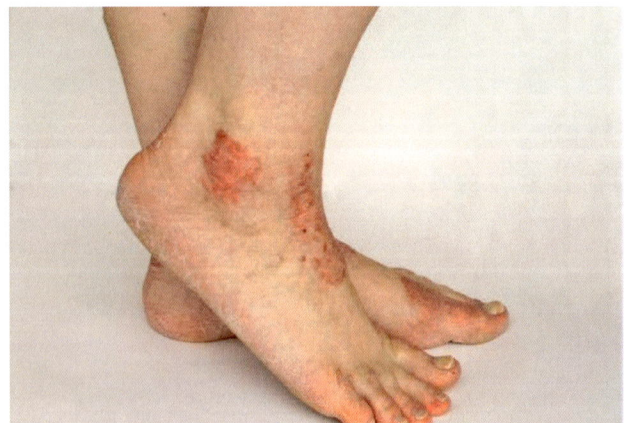

Treatments are available to manage symptoms.

Precaution: Check well that there are no open lesions in the patches of psoriasis on the skin. No treatment can be performed on an area of open lesions.

Psoriasis of the skin is painful and itchy

56

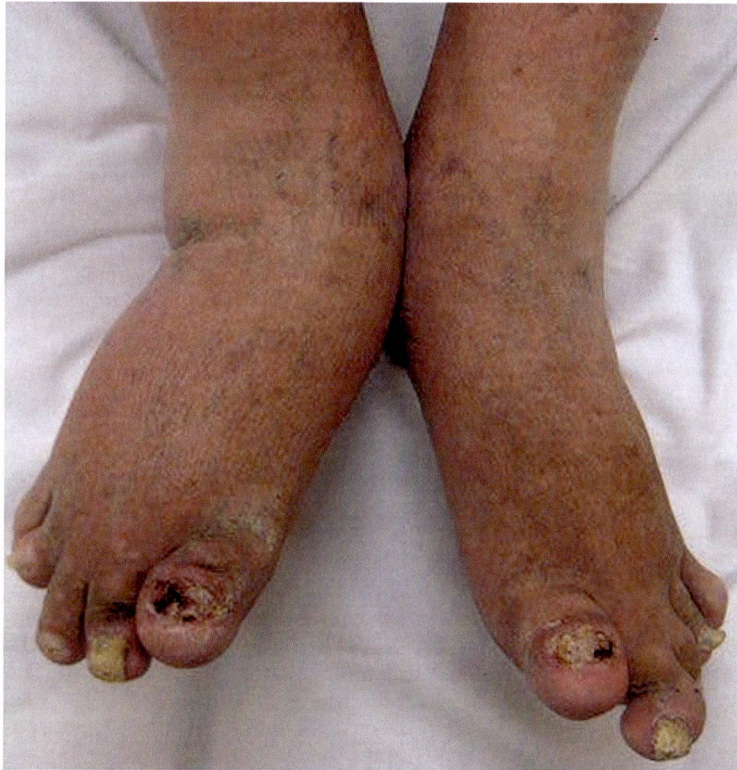

Another form of psoriasis is on the nails and is termed Psoriatic Arthritis.

Pedicurists must be aware of the serious affects these conditions can have on their clients and commit to their careful care. Adhering to precautions tightly is stressed in their care. Knowledge and gentleness are important qualities in performing safe foot care on these special clients and can alleviate most concerns in working with them.

Melanoma of the Hands and Feet: Melanoma, a rare skin disease, is considered the most serious type of skin cancer due to its rapid spread through the lymph system. Detecting melanoma on the foot is challenging, leading to a higher mortality rate than most cancers. Nail professionals should educate themselves about the visual ABCDE symptoms of skin cancer and routinely check client's hands and feet. When suspicious areas are observed, immediate referral to a physician or podiatrist is essential.

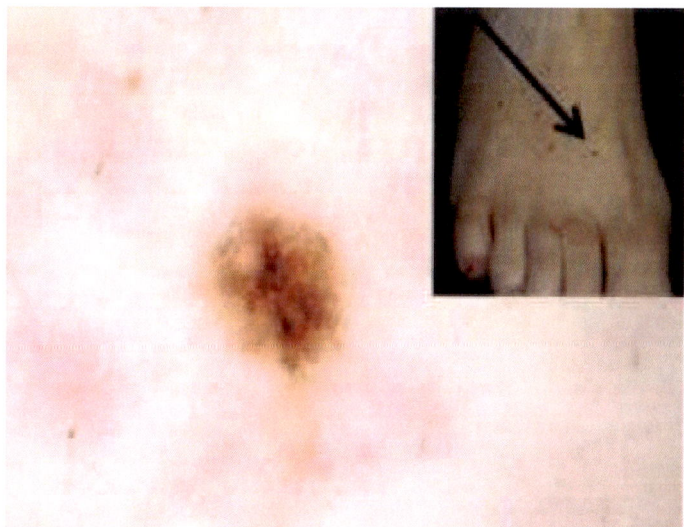

Melanoma is difficult to diagnose on visual examination and assumption by a nail professional can be dangerous for the client. Sending a client to get a lesion checked can save a life.

Infections

Infections are transferable between persons; conditions are not.

Nail professionals must refrain from performing services on infected, inflamed, or an injury of the skin or nails (the three "I's"). However, diagnosing infections is beyond their scope. Nail professionals should consider whether it is an infection, a non-infectious condition, discoloration, fungus, or pseudomonas. Referral to a physician or podiatrist is advisable when indicated.

Damaged nails are often misdiagnosed for infections. For example, psoriatic nails are frequently thought to be fungal; discolorations are also commonly misidentified as fungal infections, damage or bruises. Nail professionals are advised to avoid diagnosing conditions and to refer clients to a physician or podiatrist for a definitive diagnosis. However, the accuracy of lab tests for onychomycosis (nail fungus) is reported to be only 60-80%. This presents a challenge for nail professionals in determining how to proceed with treatment.

When you notice a questionable spot on a nail, you may wonder if it is an infection. Here is what some nail technicians do:
1. Ask the client if a physician has examined the area. If yes, and it has been diagnosed, the technician must follow state law to determine if they can work on the nail.
2. If the client has not seen a physician, the technician may perform a soakless service, isolate the area, use disposable implements on the nail last, throw them away and then recommend the client see a physician. An anti-fungal product may be suggested for use until the appointment.
3. If a full foot infection like Tinea Pedis (athlete's foot) is suspected, no service should be performed until a physician evaluates the client.
4. Never work in a client with an obvious "I" – Infection, Inflammation, or Injury.

Lori Holloway, the Meticulous Manicurist from Surprise, AZ contacted every state board in the US to inquire, "Can nail technicians work on fungal nails?" Out of the fifty state boards, 25 responded thus far, and their overall answer was... "We do not address fungus in our regulations." Nail professionals are encouraged to contact their specific state board or check their website for regulations regarding fungal nails. However, keep in mind that licensed nail professionals are not allowed to work on clients with infections, no matter their name.

Training is available for nail professionals on this topic, and it is recommended that they seek out this information. Only the most common infections are mentioned here briefly.

Athlete's Foot (Tinea Pedis) – This common fungal infection of the skin on the feet is challenging to diagnose and treat. The skin may appear flaky with closed or dried blisters. If no tiny blisters are present, it might be mistaken for dry skin, leading to exfoliation and hydration by the nail professional. However, if large flaky areas and closed blistering are observed, the client should be referred to a physician, and no service should be performed, as it may exacerbate the infection.

Note: Tinea Pedis thrives in moist environments, and moisturizing can worsen the infection. An anti-fungal lotion is recommended until the client can see a podiatrist. If the toes and nails are not involved, a nail grooming service can be performed with precautions such as gloves and disposable or autoclavable implements.

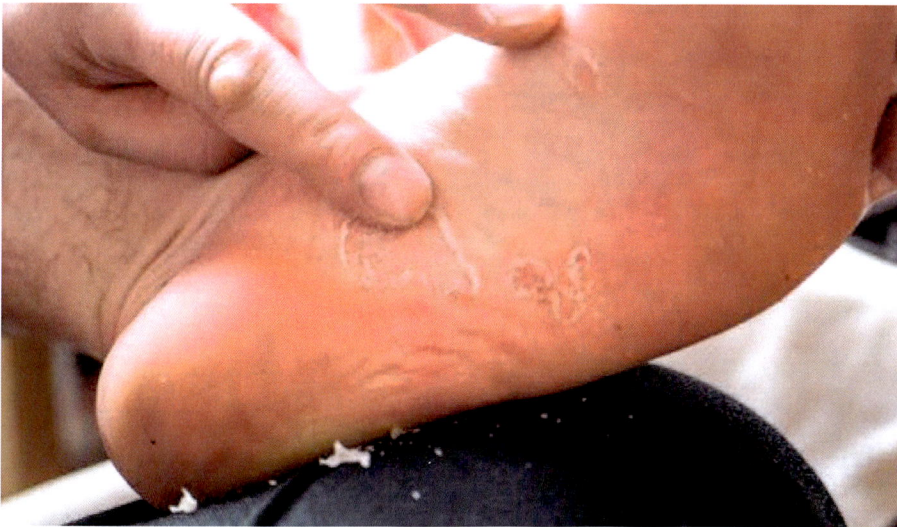

Athletes Foot (Tines Pedis) is a fungal infection of th skin, and is considered one of the most common infections in humans.

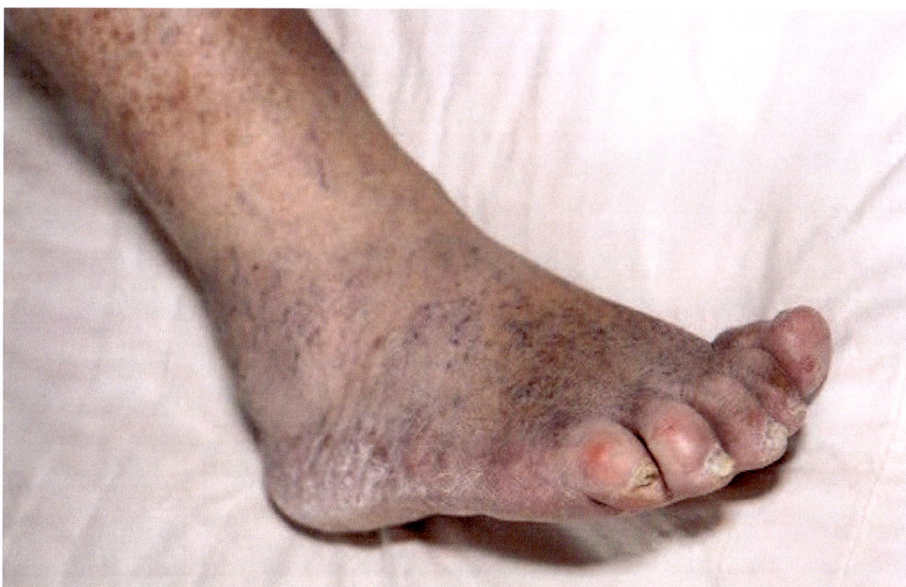

It is very contagious, but also is very difficult to control or cure. It also varies widely in appearance and so it is difficult to diagnose visually.

Cause: Dermatophytes. It can affect the skin without affecting the nails, or both, though rarely.

Onychomycosis – This fungal infection affects fingernails and toenails and is often confused with psoriasis, injury, or other conditions. Clients should be advised to visit a podiatrist for feet, a dermatologist for hands and use an anti-fungal nail treatment until the appointment. Services on unaffected feet and toes can be performed, with isolation of the infected toes until the end of the appointment.

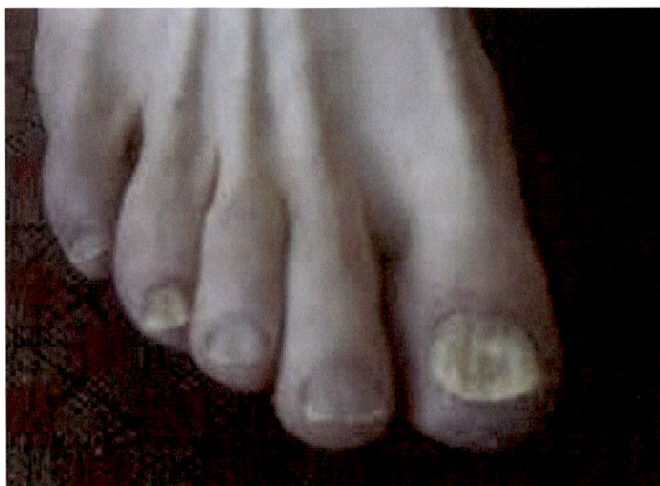

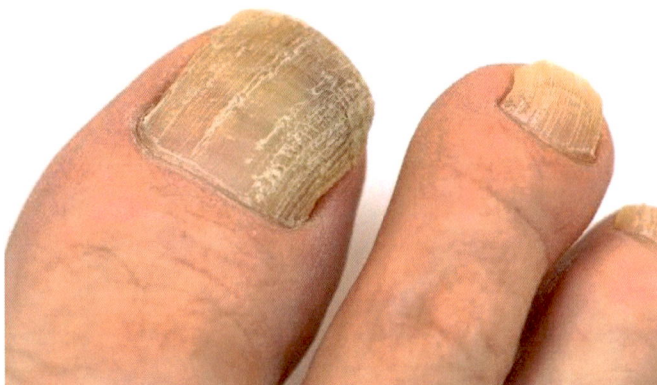

Onychomychosis – Fungus can also cause an infection of the nails. It is also very contagious and difficult to diagnose and cure.

Cause: Dermatophytes. This infection can affect the nails without affecting the skin, or both, though rarely.

Onycholysis – This condition involves the nail plate separating from the nail bed without reattachment. If the cause is injury, it requires the growth of a new nail, which takes 4-6 months. Common on the great toe, nail professionals can carefully remove the loose nail plate, clean the area, and apply a prosthetic toenail to prevent fungal and bacterial invasion.

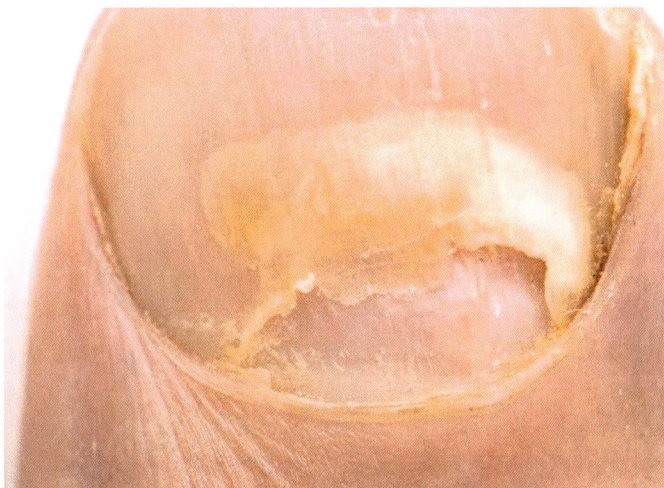

Onycholysis: In the case of damage, the nail usually grows out under the damaged nail.

In the case of the cause being the early stages of a type of fungus, it may just initially appear to be "lifting."

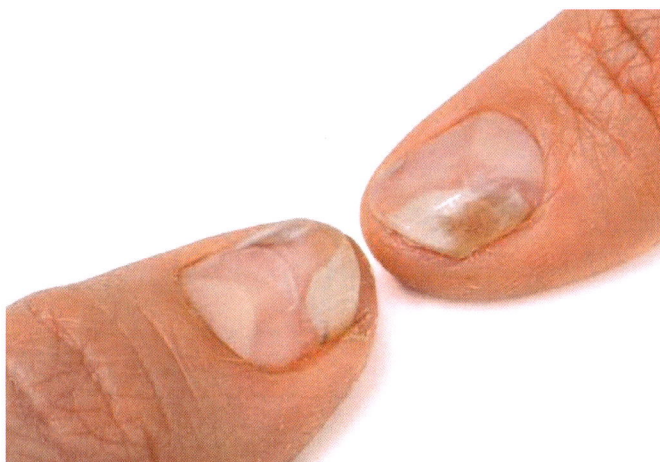

In the case of allergy or early fungal nail, the nail may have a pocket under the nail.

Cause: It may be caused by nail injury, fungus, psoriasis, illness, medications or even tight shoes. The condition persists until a new nail grows.

Pseudomonas aeruginosa – Pseudomonas is an opportunistic pathogen that can infect various body parts but is of particular interest to nail professionals when it occurs on or under real or artificial nails. These bacteria thrive in damp environments with little oxygen. On nails, P. aeruginosa causes green nail syndrome (chromonychia), or "greenies", which can alarm nail professionals and clients. However, there is no need to panic—greenies can be treated effectively if caught early. If a slight green tint is observed under enhancements or on nail plates after enhancement removal, clean the area and remove the green stain immediately before the bacteria penetrates the nail plate. Use an emery or buffer to remove as much green as possible, then apply 61%-91% alcohol to the area, allowing it to dry thoroughly between at least two applications. A quality dehydrator should then be used. Whether to reapply product or polish is a decision for the experienced nail technician.

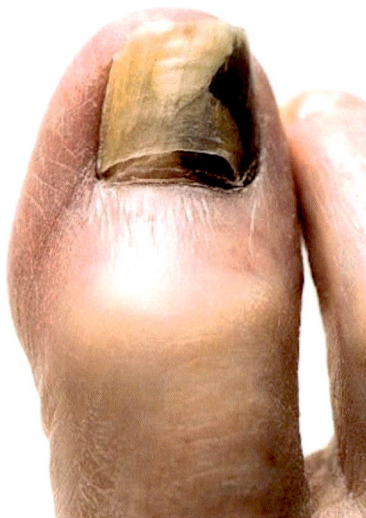

Pseudomonas aeruginosa is a bacterial infection that can occur on both the skin and nails.
Usually in an area where little oxygen is available.

If *P. aeruginosa* growth is unchecked, it progresses from light green to dark green, then brown to black. When it reaches dark green, it is time to refer the client to a physician for potential topical or oral treatment. Never apply an enhancement over this infection until it has been treated and the innocuous stain is growing off.

To prevent greenies, nail professionals must maintain sanitary conditions and apply enhancements correctly to avoid trapping microbes. Enhancements should never be applied to a damp nail plate. After prepping, avoid having the client wash their hands; instead, wipe off residue with alcohol or dehydrator before proceeding with the service. Dampness is a breeding ground for microbes.

Aseptic practices are crucial to prevent the spread of infections. Nail professionals should always assume every client is infected and work to prevent disease transmission. Assuming a client is not infected could jeopardize the health of subsequent clients and the nail professional.

Chapter 8

Customized Protocols

Every analysis leads to a recommendation and the performance of a service that is customized to meet the needs of the client being served at that moment. Then, the recommended treatment is integrated into the basic protocol, elevating it to a higher level of custom care. For this reason, nail professionals are encouraged to first master the basic soakless manicures and pedicures until they can perform them by rote, without thinking about "what comes next." Afterward, they can transition to skincare-based services by adding the appropriate treatment.

Suggestion: Practice services support growth of professional confidence before moving into paid services. Then, copy the soakless procedure in short form (See Appendix), place it inside a plastic cover, and bring it to the mani-table/pedi-chair as a reference. It is best if the client does not see the professional referring to it, so it should be positioned out of the client's view.

Basic Soakless Manicure and Pedicure

The distinction between traditional basic manicures and pedicures and the skincare based basic ones lies in the protocol. This soakless skincare version is designed to produce more vibrant and glowing skin, and provide more relaxation, even though the service is "basic."

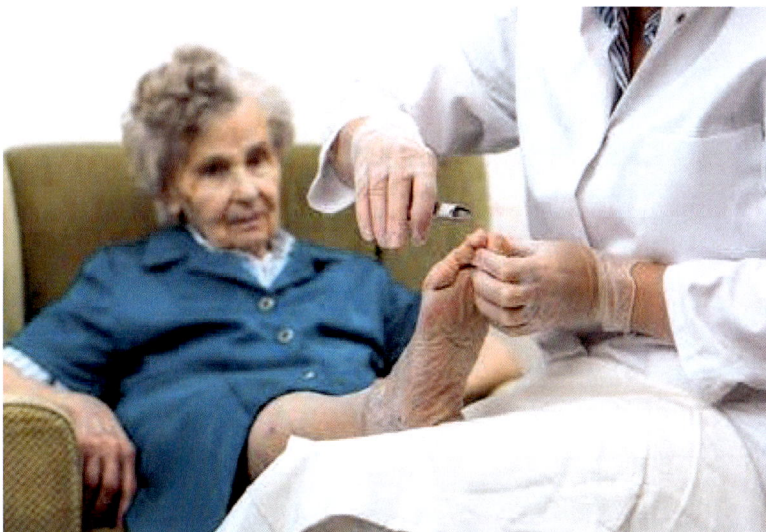

A soakless pedicure has many advantages, but to many chronically ill clients, it is the only pedicure they can have.

Refer to the protocol in the Appendix.

The soakless method includes three massages: the first during cleansing, the second during the scrub treatment, and the third is the traditional or modified massage. Each has its unique characteristics, but they all constitute a form of massage and should be presented as such to the client to enhance their perception of the service.

Cleansing Massage: The cleansing massage is performed on the hand if the pre-service sink cleansing is not performed; it is always performed on the feet. Performed after the initial observation of the area's condition, the cleansing gel is typically dispensed with two to three pumps into a hand, then spread around the hand or foot to cleanse. Gentle pressure is applied in a patterned, massage-type application. The choice of cleansing product is up to the nail professional, but many find that a hand cleansing gel (pumped from a no label dispenser) provides the appropriate slip for the massage motions while performing an excellent cleanse. Remove the remaining gel with a warm, wet towel.

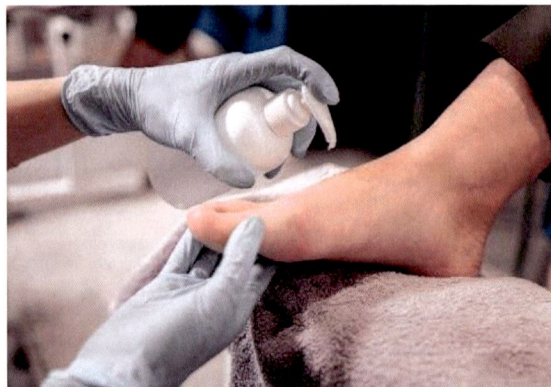

The soakless cleanser should be in a pump bottle with no brand label.

Exfoliation (Scrub) Massage: Apply the scrub product and manipulate it around the treatment area. Usually, one minute per hand or foot is sufficient to achieve this while giving the impression of a true massage.

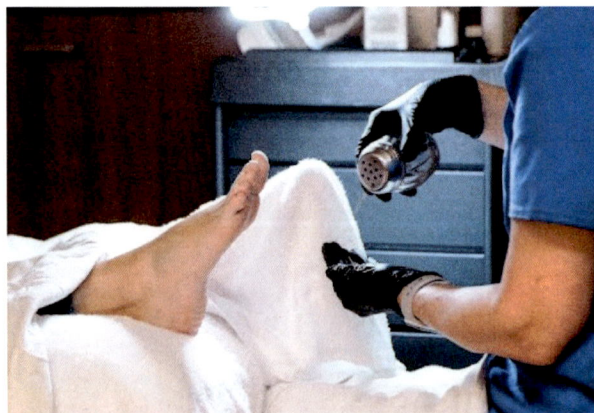

Utilizing a gentle scrub is in the protocol prepares the skin for penetration of th ingredients of the treatment products.

In skincare-based services, a gentle scrub product with granules that will not scratch the skin is used to dislodge and remove dead cells and debris from the skin's surface. Eliminating the barrier allows for increased penetration of ingredients from the treatment products. It is ideal to find a product with granules for exfoliation that will dissolve during application, eliminating the need for removal. If such a product cannot be sourced, the scrub must be removed before applying the massage lotion.

Relaxation Massage: This is the massage clients look forward to in the service. A pattern of even, relaxing, slow movements should be established (no deep massage

Suggestion: Learn to keep one hand on the skin while dispensing more product by using a product with a pump. Hook the thumb of the reaching hand over the pump and press it down to dispense onto the inside of your fingers.

– that is beyond our scope of practice) that may even lull the client to sleep. In treatment services, a good hydrating lotion with high-quality ingredients is used for the massage because the scrub has removed the oils. However, hydrating lotions will require reapplication during the massage movements. Traditional massage lotions/ oils are barrier products; they coat the skin and do not penetrate quickly, allowing them to last longer during the massage. Their function is to provide and maintain abundant slip, not to treat the skin through penetration. In contrast, skincare-based services aim for penetration to rehydrate the skin, as well as to perform a relaxing massage.

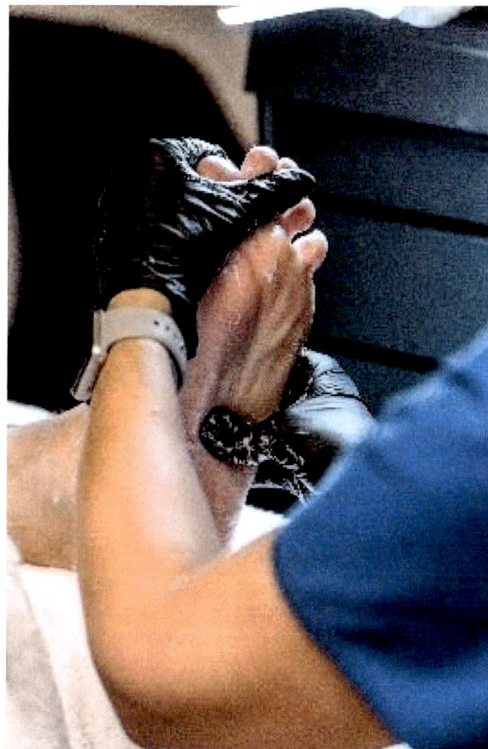

The product for massage in a treatment protocol should be a penetrating lotion, not a barrier lotion.

Treatment Services

The analysis and consultation are crucial for recommending the appropriate service and discussing necessary home care. Agreement to perform the recommended service must always be obtained before proceeding.

> **Always Suggesting Upgrades**
> Avoid becoming known for consistently suggesting upgrades. Customization is advised only when indicated through analysis. Recommending an occasional upgrade, such as a hydrating pedicure for its pampering and luxury, is acceptable without implying a skin necessity if there is not one.

To secure this agreement, the technician must explicitly ask for it. For example, "Based on what I see today, shall we proceed with the treatment we discussed? [Yes or no] That will be an additional $xx." Instead of stating the new price, it is suggested to mention the upgrade amount. For instance, rather than saying, "Your service will be $55," say, "That will be $10 more for your service."

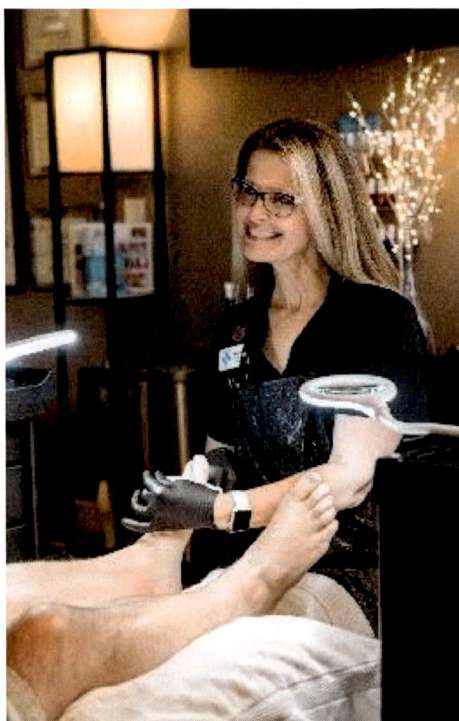

Always gain approval for upgrade before proceeding

These recommended services address conditions noted during the analysis. Each incorporates a specific treatment into the basic protocol to target the client's condition. For ongoing skin improvement, clients must perform home care, and the nail professional should discuss this constructive collaboration during recommendations. During the initial appointment, educate the client about the partnership being formed to address the treatment issue: the professional tackles the condition with an intensive service during the salon visit, while the client's recommended home care extends and enhances the results.

It is best to briefly mention home care and its importance during the consultation, then elaborate during the service. For example, "This is the lotion you'll need to apply nightly at home. It contains [hyaluronic acid], which ....," and explain the ingredient's benefits.

After mastering the basic protocol, it is time to incorporate the treatment as determined during the analysis/consultation.

Discussion of the protocols for each service follow. All protocols are based on the basic service with the treatments add as upgrades. Some eliminate a step, such as the massage during the mature skin treatment. Close attention should be given to the protocol for each specialty manicure or pedicure.

Basic Soakless Manicure and Pedicure

This service contains the following steps: Analysis, Cleansing, Scrub, Massage, Cuticle and Callus Treatments, Moisturization, Finish and Close. The protocol is listed in the Appendix in copyable form, plus a short form protocol to take to the station, if desired. All higher-level treatment services are based on this service.

Scrub Manicure and Pedicure

This service is the basic manicure/pedicure with an enhanced scrub step. When clients have dry, scaly skin on their hands and feet, the upgraded scrub treatment extends up the arms and/or legs, and home care follows suit. Always include these areas in the upgraded scrub manicure or pedicure, as they are often dry and scaly too, and this extension justifies the higher cost—always more than the basic service, which may only focus on the hands or feet.

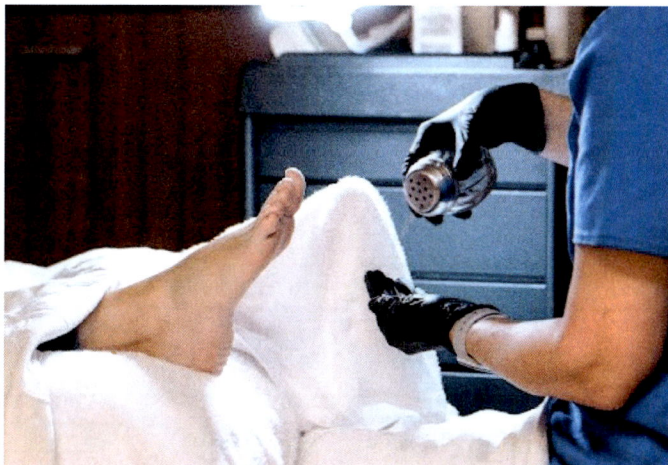

Utilizing a gentle scrub is in the protocol prepares the skin for penetration of th ingredients of the treatment products.

Home Care: A good-quality lotion for ongoing home use is essential, along with a gentle scrub home care product to be used twice weekly following instructions. Some clients may require a low AHA lotion twice weekly to enhance the release of dead cells, but this should not be used on the same night as the scrub product.

Home care for this treatment includes the hydrating SPF lotion for daytime use and a 4-9% AHA lotion for nightly or bi-weekly application, considering the sensitivity of the skin.

Hydrating Manicures and Pedicures.

This service is the basic manicure/pedicure, including a light scrub and a hydration treatment. The hydration treatment is added into the basic manicure after the relaxation massage. See the Appendix for the protocol. This service can be enhanced through the addition of paraffin over the hydration product plus terry cloth mitts, or the addition of plastic foot covers and electric mitts over the hydration mask or product. Additional support items such as drinks, candies, cookies, and candles enhance the pampering and luxurious experience, bringing it into being the spa signature service.

Aromatherapy Manicures and Pedicures:

These manicures and pedicures follow the spa manicure and pedicure protocols but incorporate synergistic (same aroma) aromatherapy products throughout. Due to the higher cost of products, amenities and the extended time required, this service is priced higher. It is particularly well-suited for spa packages.

An Aromatherapy Manicure/Pedicure is a luxurious and soothing service many enjoy in high end spas.

Home care products for this treatment are the same as those for the Hydrating Manicure and Pedicure.

Anti-Aging Manicure and Pedicure:

Anti-aging manicures and pedicures involve strategic treatment planning, usually comprising a series of services. Clients must commit to weekly manicures and/or treatments as part of a program aimed at achieving long-term results. These treatments address concerns such as wrinkles, dehydration, dryness, or hyperpigmentation. Pedicures are typically performed weekly or bi-weekly, depending on the client's specific needs. Clients who adhere to this program can expect their hands and feet to appear younger, with improved tone, texture and a more even, youthful glow. The results are highly satisfying.

To achieve anti-aging goals, it is crucial to use high-quality products. This involves researching product ingredients and understanding their precautions.

Treatment: The anti-aging treatment includes chemical exfoliants, lightening agents, hydration, and SPF. The service is based on the basic manicure/pedicure, with anti-aging treatments added. However, since the professional product is a chemical exfoliant (AHA), the traditional massage is excluded. (Massage stimulation can cause skin redness and excessive penetration of the liquid.) See the Appendix for the protocol.

The AHA lotion used for this treatment follows a different protocol than liquid AHA and is preferred by most nail technicians. The actual treatment involves a 15-20% AHA lotion. Conducting a patch test for the exfoliation product after client acceptance but before treatment is recommended.

Any remaining product should be removed with a wet towel if it has not fully penetrated, followed by the application of a hydration lotion. Important: Heat, such as paraffin or warm mitts, is not involved in this treatment to prevent penetration that can be harmful to the client. If desired, the hand/arm or foot/leg can be wrapped in a cool towel post-treatment.

The duration of the AHA lotion massage varies: three minutes during the first treatment, increasing by one minute per subsequent treatment, up to a maximum of five-seven minutes. For clients with sensitivity (not indicated in the patch test), the massage should never exceed 3-5 minutes. After removal of the AHA product, the hydrating lotion remains on the treatment area, and SPF is applied at the end of the treatment.

Home Care: In this program, lotions and treatment products play a crucial role. A gentle scrub and chemical exfoliating lotion with lower AHAs (up to 9%) are essential, as is a moisturizing lotion with SPF. If lentigines (dark spots) are present, a brightening home care product is also vital. The exfoliation lotion is always used in the evening as the last product applied.

Timing for the AHA Lotion and Scrubs

Proper timing must be taught to prevent overuse of the AHA lotion and scrubs. The scrub should be used twice a week, while the AHA lotion, containing 4-9% AHAs, is to be used every night, depending on the client's skin sensitivity. For heavy calluses and anti-aging, a higher concentration of AHA in the lotion can be used two or three times weekly.

Ingredients for Anti-Aging

The professional exfoliation treatment product, whether lotion or liquid, typically includes glycolic acid—an alpha hydroxy acid—at a concentration of 15%-20% for these services. The lotion is specifically designated for hand use. Home products contain lactic acid and other AHAs at a lower strength, up to 9%. Retinoids may also be included in the formulation. Hydration products often feature hyaluronic acid at concentrations of 3-10%, the highest form of hydration available, along with soothing ingredients and antioxidants for anti-aging. Good anti-aging lotions usually contain anti-aging peptides, which are short-chain proteins designed to stimulate collagen and elastine development.

If sourcing products within the nail industry proves challenging, one can look to facial and hand products from the skincare industry, paying close attention to the percentages of treatment products as mentioned above.

(See the protocol in the Appendix.)

Many skin and nail salons place the lotion products to be used during a service on an art palate in the order of use to 1) save time and movements in attaining the products during the service, and to 2) conserve use of products during the service. If prepared early in the day, it is covered with plastic wrap to maintain freshness until the service.

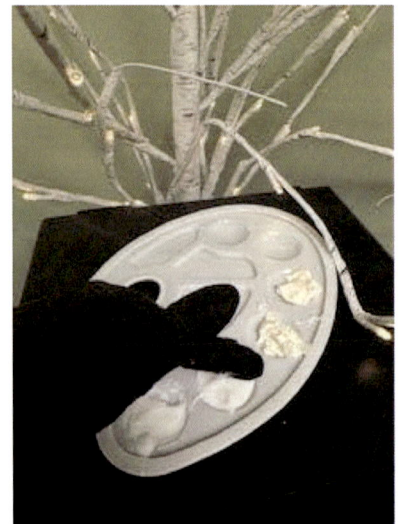

Treatment for Anti-Aging While Performing Enhancements

Enhancement clients deserve anti-aging also. Apply the treatment exfoliation lotion and massage it into one hand for one to two minutes prior to the enhancement service, leaving it on the hand. Then, at the proper time, apply the hydration lotion liberally and massage into the skin. (This lotion will neutralize the AHA lotion.) Fingerless gloves can be worn to enhance the treatment after applying the hydrating lotion. Prepare the nails and proceed with the enhancement treatment. Next, perform the exfoliation treatment on the other hand and then apply the AHA treatment to this hand in a massage motion and place the fingers in the glove (optional). Proceed as with the other hand.

Some product lines have protocols set up for performing skin care during application of their enhancement products. They are designed to fit their treatment philosophy.

An alternative method is to prepare one hand, apply the exfoliating lotion, and then move to preparing and applying it to the second hand. The "set" time must be watched closely for neutralizing the exfoliant. Usually, application to the second hand is just enough time to return to the first hand to begin the enhancement service. Then, neutralizing the second hand must interrupt the enhancements being applied to the first hand at the proper time, and then the hand is laid aside for its enhancement step after completing the first hand.

An SPF hydrating lotion is applied to both hands at the end of the service. The use of SPF is crucial for ongoing results, as is the client's use during the day at home and work. Without SPF use, results will not be achieved.

Be vigilant for any enhanced redness of the skin after the treatment is applied. If the skin begins to turn pink, remove the gloves and the product immediately. Involve the client in monitoring for sensitivities, advising them, "If your skin begins to redden or prickle, tell me at once so I can remove the treatment."

Take care to avoid applying lotions to the nail bed area. With careful application, exfoliation lotion can be applied to calluses, etc., without being on the nail bed area.

Routine Home Care for Anti-Aging

Evening use: Twice weekly use a gentle scrub and after removal, a hydrating lotion. Other nights, the low percentage exfoliating lotion is applied. It is also hydrating.

Morning and daily repeat use: SPF hydrating lotion after washing hands.

Sunspots on the Hands and Feet

Baby boomers have embraced skincare to help them look and feel younger, and it has been effective... for the face. They are aware that they can make their faces appear younger, but their hands can betray their age. For that reason, many seek a nail professional who is willing to learn and perform services that will anti-age their hands. Combine this with offering effective home care products and this nail professional's appointment book will be full, with a waiting list.

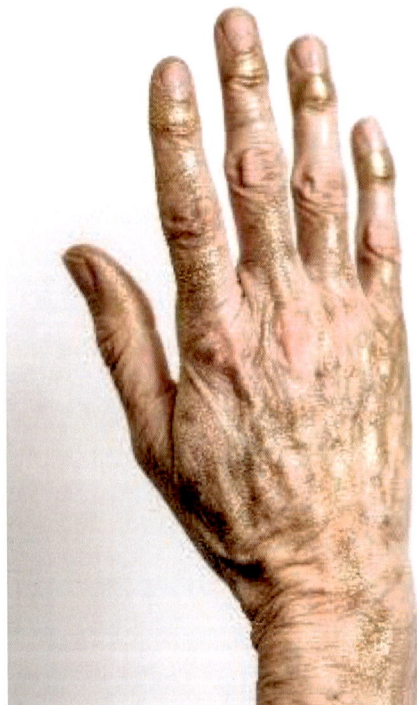

Hyperpigmentation is the plague of the elderly.

Dark Spots and Hyperpigmentation

Dark spots, also known as hyperpigmentation, are usually flat, brown-to-black discolorations of the skin that often appear in patches on the back of the hands, face, back, decollete and other areas. They are harmless and are commonly associated with aging and sun damage, though they can have other causes as well. This condition is known by many names, with the official name being 'solar lentigines.' One type, melasma, is spots caused by hormonal imbalances during pregnancy, menopause, or while taking birth control, leading to damage, and darkening of the melanocytes; the result is dark spots.

All solar lentigines are caused by overexposure to UV rays from the sun. Many clients call them liver spots, a misnomer as these spots are not related to liver conditions. Freckles, a form of hyperpigmentation, develop from site-specific sensitivity to UV exposure due to a genetic propensity for overproduction of melanin in the area.

Nail professionals should become proficient in treatments for these spots, as they are a common concern among people who wish to appear younger; they will ask, "Can you get rid of these for me?" The answer: "No, but we can minimize them and keep them from becoming larger and darker." Treatments such as exfoliation with AHAs and retinoids, often combined with light therapy and skin brighteners, can lighten the spots. However, these treatments must be supported by consistent and ongoing home care. Lifelong adherence to 'skin brightening' products and the use of SPF lotions is crucial. Clients should be aware that even one day of excessive sun exposure can reverse progress, necessitating a restart of the treatment.

Understanding hyperpigmentation is essential for nail professionals offering this care. It is caused by darkened, damaged melanocytes that respond by overproducing melanin, the natural pigment in the skin. These melanocytes are in the basal layer of the skin and can become damaged by factors such as sun exposure, medications, injuries, and more.

Melanocytes are specialized cells that produce melanin to protect cell nuclei and DNA from UV radiation damage. However, they can become easily damaged, leading to an overproduction of melanin and the appearance of hyperpigmentation as the melanin moves through the skin layers. While it is challenging to completely fade these spots, they can be dramatically reduced over time.

The practice of lightening skin coloration was once referred to as 'skin bleaching', typically performed with products containing hydroquinone. However, many countries have moved away from this term and now use 'skin brighteners.' The term skin brighteners is believed to moderate expectations for lightening of the skin and is now used in referring to treatment and home care lotions containing ingredients which interfere with the darkening of the melanocytes. These ingredients will not bleach the skin but will lighten it over time.

Hydroquinone has been banned in many countries for over-the-counter sales, and prescriptions are restricted in concentration. This is because federal agencies, such as the FDA in the US, have determined that hydroquinone has not met the standards of GRAS (Generally Regarded As Safe). This follows bans in other countries like Japan, Australia, and Europe, where it was prohibited due to its toxicity to melanocytes. Some physicians argue that hydroquinone is safe if used as directed for a limited time (usually four months) and monitored for overuse.

In the event of overuse, hydroquinone can cause a condition known as *ochronosis*, characterized by papules and bluish-black pigmentation on the skin surface. These changes can be permanent and are typically found in Africa, though there have been a few diagnoses in the USA. Ochronosis is extremely difficult to treat once diagnosed. The physical and emotional suffering from this condition is intense.

Physician-prescribed hydroquinone concentrations are usually between 2-4%, with close monitoring and a four-month limitation on use. This period is followed by a break from the product before potentially renewing the treatment for the same duration. Prescriptions are 2-4%, though compounded formulations of 6%-8% can be created under prescription by compounding laboratories. One concern physicians have regarding the banning of low-percentage products is their availability from unscrupulous foreign companies, which can be easily ordered on the internet.

Alternatives to Hydroquinone

There are alternative ingredients available in formulations that are effective as skin brighteners, these ingredients are called tyrosinase-inhibitors, they are ingredients that prevent the melanin in the skin from being produced, or reduce the activity. These 'hydroquinone-free' lightening agent ingredients include vitamin C, retinoids, kojic acid, ellagic acid, lactic acid, azelaic acid, glycolic acid, licorice root, retinaldehyde, salicylic acid, niacinamide, and tranexamic acid in combination formulations. Unfortunately, they are currently only available to aestheticians in the professional beauty market, though this is changing. However, a nail care company is set to launch a full line for nail technicians and many companies are expected to follow. The line will include an exfoliator lotion, a skin brightener, and SPF products, fulfilling a long-standing need in the nail industry. In the meantime, order the products from skin care companies.

Dark Spots

Increased melanin production unrelated to sun exposure can also occur in rare conditions such as Addison's and Cushing's diseases.

Light Therapy

Light therapy is utilized in anti-aging and hyperpigmentation therapies, as well as in pain relief treatments. LED light therapy (light-emitting diode) in the red spectrum addresses aging and dark spots on sun-exposed surfaces of the body. The red and amber spectrums are anti-inflammatory, also, and can provide quick pain relief, making them suitable for clients with arthritis.

Salons can offer LED light therapy as an add-on in treatments with hand-held lights or as a 'drop-in' treatment for a fee while a standalone light device is positioned over the treatment area.

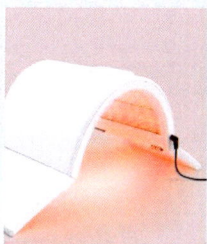

Educated clients appreciate the benefits of LED therapy and enjoy the opportunity for a quiet respite while their hyperpigmentation is treated. This treatment does not require a professional to be present and has no known negative side effects.

LED therapy involves safe, visible, and infrared light wavelengths applied to the skin from a handpiece or standalone device. The light penetrates the skin epidermis at various depths depending on the wavelength used. The light stimulates fibroblasts, supporting the production of natural enzymes that increase collagen production, enhance healing, reduce inflammation, and dark spots, and improve skin tone and texture. According to both NASA and the FDA, LED light has been scientifically proven to promote healing and effectively treat wrinkles, and to lighten hyperpigmentation. It is non-invasive, does not include harmful UV rays, and can be used regularly. No negative side effects are known.

Colored light is produced when the particles that carry the current combine within the semiconductor material and become excited. Red LED light is proven to improve circulation, stimulate the production of collagen and elastin, reduce inflammation, and lighten hyperpigmentation, while amber LED light diminishes pain and reduces inflammation, which contributes to aging. Most treatment lights now combine these spectrums to increase their effectiveness. Results are typically seen after a series of treatments scheduled at regular intervals, complemented by home care. A single treatment is unlikely to show dramatic results, but several weeks of regular treatments, accompanied by diligent home care, can show marked improvement in wrinkles and sunspots.

It is important to manage clients' expectations by explaining that the dark color may initially worsen as it 'rises' from its origin in the damaged melanocytes but will improve as the light treats the birth layer and the darkened cells are exfoliated. Taking a 'before' and 'after' picture of the hands with similar lighting can help clients see the dramatic difference. Many clients report seeing a significant improvement at around 8-12 weeks, depending on the severity of their condition.

Currently, LCN's Studio System is the only comprehensive treatment in the nail industry for anti-aging and reduction of hyperpigmentation. It includes an exfoliating mask and effective lotions containing urea and lactic acid, used along with a Light Therapy implement that emits LED therapy light. A light unit and supportive products are also available at Centre of Beauty, Largo, Florida. Other lights are available in the skincare industry.

> **Light Therapy**
>
> Light therapy is a painless treatment that can be added to any manicure or pedicure or other treatment to enhance results for anti-aging and pain relief. LED red is anti-inflammatory. This treatment is very hands-on for both the technician and client and is considered a high-end service.

Callus Control Manicure and Pedicure

The goal of this treatment is to reduce calluses and to slow or prevent their return. It is often the most recommended treatment and series in the nail department. The protocol can also be used in manicures for heavy callusing.

Treatment: This manicure and pedicure involve the application of callus softeners and the use of a pedi-paddle or e-file to address calluses. Some nail professionals perform an AHA treatment on the calluses to soften them before using the pedi-paddle or e-file. However, there are excellent callus softeners available now that are highly effective for these services.

For heavy calluses, a series of treatments will reduce the calluses gradually, allowing the skin to adjust to the reduced protection and not respond with a rapid replenishment of the calluses. When calluses are removed too quickly, as with illegal blades, the skin responds by quickly producing more callus to protect the area, negating the benefit of removal.

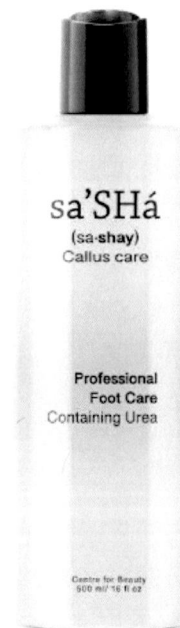

sa'SHá
(sa-shay)
Callus care

Professional
Foot Care
Containing Urea

Centre for Beauty
500 ml/ 16 fl oz

Apply callus soften only to the calluses and leave only for the instructed time, then remove.

Home Care: Clients must use a low AHA lotion nightly and a pedi-paddle after showering as recommended by the nail professional to reduce the regeneration of calluses. The frequency of pedi-paddle use will be determined by the nail professional but is typically weekly or bi-weekly.

> Remember, do not become aggressive during either the callus pedicures or treatments in removing the callusing as, 1) the feet may become sore, 2) the calluses may be stimulated to regenerate quickly, countering the benefit of slow reduction, and 3) sticking to the time allotted for the pedicure or treatment is very important. The reasons for slow removal should be explained to clients,

Careful Callus Removal

Heavy calluses respond well to a Callus Control Series, which can dramatically reduce their continued presence. The full pedicure is not performed during treatment services between monthly pedicures. A Callus Control Treatment is performed in much less time, with a half-hour appointment recommended. The price is more than half of the pedicure price.

Refer to the manicure and pedicure protocol for Callus Control in the Appendix, as well as the treatments performed in the Callus Control series.

> **Success Contribution**
>
> The Callus Control Pedicure and treatment series can contribute to the success of a nail professional and provide significant growth to a clientele. This protocol should be learned immediately following the incorporation of the Soakless Pedicure to a nail professional's menu. Recruiting a friend with heavy calluses as a practice series demonstrates well the results and provides before and after photos to show future clients.

Nail Growth Treatment

This treatment involves adding a massage of the nail matrix area within any manicure or pedicure service to stimulate the growth of the nail plate. This massage can dramatically increase the growth rate and condition of the nails.

Treatment: Perform the manicure according to the skincare condition, and include a matrix massage after the hand and arm massage. Be certain you separate this massage activity from the hand and arm massage. One method to draw attention to it is by asking if the pressure is appropriate during the massage. Another is teaching the mechanics of it to the client for home care use.

Train the client to perform this massage on the matrix area of the nail beds as well as on the nail folds and nail beds. Toenails that grow slowly can also benefit from daily matrix massages, though results may not be as immediate.

Home Care: Apply an oil or treatment product, then clients massage the nail from side to side on the matrix using medium pressure. It is important to note that the pad of the thumb is not used for the massage; instead, use the side of the thumb joint (knuckle).

Grow-off Manicures

This basic manicure allows the product on the surface of the nail to grow off naturally while protecting the nail underneath. Clients must visit weekly for about 3 weeks or more. During each visit, enhancements are shortened, and the product is thinned at the free edge until it eventually lifts off. The stress point is moved back to the proper position behind the hyponychium. Always cleanse the nail and any loosened area with an alcohol product, allow it to dry, then thin the area to flattened edges. Do not allow the drill to move onto the nail bed. When the nail is completely dry, glue any loose edges to the nail to prevent bacteria and fungus from entering.

Any area of product release is removed, cleansed with alcohol, and a nail treatment is performed for two to three or more weeks during the service, by the professional. After all the nail product is released, treat the full nail surface with the treatment product during each manicure, allowing the nails to return to their normal hydration and strength. A home care nail treatment and matix massage product are also important.

Clients appreciate this method of returning to natural nails because it minimizes tearing of the free edge and quickly results in healthy nails with a good free edge.

This technique requires practice to maintain good-looking nails during the grow-off period, but once mastered, few nail professionals revert to soak-off or e-file removal. A higher price is charged for the manicure, typically $10 per service above the standard service, or a charge is added only for the added nail treatment. The grow-off techniques are time-efficient and safe, especially when the technician is trained and adept at using an e-file properly.

Nail Biters – A Special Group of Clients

Nail biters present a unique challenge for nail professionals. These clients often struggle with the habit of biting their nails, and addressing this behavior requires patience and tailored care. Here are some considerations and strategies for working with nail biters:

1. Understanding the Behavior:

- Nail biters may not always be aware of when or why they bite their nails. As a professional, ask questions to understand their triggers and patterns.
- Habit Reversal Training can help clients replace nail biting with alternative behaviors. For example, suggest using a small, bright red ball to squeeze while driving or during deep concentration. Also, applying a nail care treatment product can defer the urge to bite.

2. Treatment Options:

- Weekly manicures can help manage rough edges and encourage nail growth. However, consistency is key, as one bite can lead to a relapse.
- Enhancements (such as acrylic or gel overlays) can deter nail biting by changing the texture and feel of the nails. Charging for repairs on bitten enhancements reinforces the message.
- Matrix massages during regular manicures stimulate nail growth and can be effective for nail biters as a behavioral deflection from biting

3. Home Care:

- Encourage clients to apply oils or nail treatments nightly, massaging the matrix and side walls to promote growth and promote healing.
- Nail biters respond well to active participation in their treatment journey. Involve them in their own care, such as gently filing rough free edges to prevent biting.
- Home care activities can defer the nail biter from biting the nails.

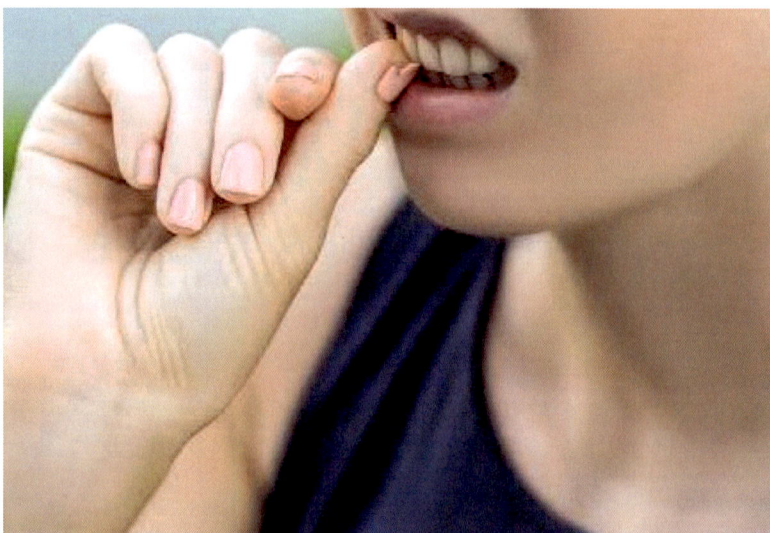

Nail biters commit to treatments by nail professionals in hopes of breaking the habit.

Nail biting can stem from a learned habit or be a symptom of underlying issues such as chronic stress or disorders like OCD (obsessive-compulsive disorder). In both cases, enhancements can serve as a valuable part of therapy. Therapists sometimes refer patients to skilled nail professionals for supportive care in managing this habit.

> **Nail Biter Therapy**
> A skilled nail professional can build a loyal clientele of former nail biters by successfully helping them quit this habit. Many nail biters genuinely want to quit, and with patience and technical expertise, professionals can guide them toward healthier nails and no biting. Some clients may choose to wear enhancements permanently to prevent relapse.
>
> Trust and consistent care are essential in supporting nail biters on their journey to beautiful, bite-free nails.

A nail professional can charge higher prices for this care. "Curing" a nail biter can be satisfying for both the professional and the client.

Manicures and Pedicures for the Elderly

Elderly clients often have delicate skin that requires gentle handling to avoid bruising or splitting. Nail professionals should use soft, slow, and careful movements with plenty of lotion during massages. A hydrating manicure with a gentle scrub is typically recommended, focusing on providing touch, pampering, and improved nail/skin appearance rather than anti-aging treatments.

The elderly cannot trim their nails on their feet usually and enjoy the pampering in well-designed manicure/pedicure protocols

Arthritic Hand and Foot Care

Clients with arthritis need special attention during manicures and pedicures. During the manicure or pedicure recommended for their skin condition, avoid any pulling movements on fingers or toes during massages to prevent joint pain. Gentle massages with the palms or gentle tapotement, and treatments like paraffin or warm mitts can offer soothing relief. Light Therapy treatments using red spectrums, and amber, if available, are also beneficial for pain relief.

Clients on Chemotherapy

When providing services to clients undergoing chemotherapy, nail professionals must exhibit the highest level of professionalism and empathy. It is crucial to communicate with clients about their care preferences and tolerance levels, which can vary depending on their treatment plan. The goal is to help these clients feel pretty, pampered, and positive during their service.

Connecting with Oncology Clients

Professionals seeking to build a rapport with oncology clients must embark on a learning journey to transition from what they "think" they know to what they "need" to know. A recommended course for nail professionals is "Oncology Care in the

Pedicure Room" at CJ's Centre for Beauty in Largo, Florida. This class provides targeted information on cancer facts, treatments, integrated therapies, and how to adapt nail services for immunocompromised clients. It emphasizes the importance of understanding the client's body, mind, and spirit to provide efficient service.

Treatments: The analysis and consultation will determine the recommended service, which often includes hydrating treatments like the hydration manicure or pedicure, as cancer treatments can be drying. Products should be fragrance-free. A discussion with the client's physician may be appropriate.

Home Care: Suggest intensely hydrating lotions that are fragrance-free and contain no irritants for the patient. Fragrance - free skincare products are available. SPF is also crucial for these clients.

Adding Custom Protocols

Custom manicures and pedicures which address conditions may not appear on service menus. Many professionals prefer to recommend them during analysis as needed, focusing on the custom aspect of their treatments. This approach allows for flexibility in service recommendations and avoids the need to explain deviations from the appointment book. It also enhances the perceived custom and therapeutic value of the service for the client. Not listing these services simplifies the process for professionals. Many list a basic pedicure and then in the description under "Custom Pedicure," or "Therapeutic Pedicures," or such, add "Our manicures and pedicures are customized according to the needs of the client's skin and nails." The price should then be listed as "$XX and up."

Special pricing and the benefits for a treatment series should be clearly communicated to the client.

Series Protocols for Pedicures

A treatment series recommended toward improving a condition such as callusing or dryness has two protocols within the services.

1. The monthly pedicure includes a full protocol of the service, from analysis to finishing.

2. The treatment services weekly or bi-weekly between the monthly pedicures only contain the cleansing, product application and set time, the core care and lotion applied. It takes less than half the time.

3. The appointment time is usually a half hour while charges are more than half the usual charge for the regular service.

4. If the client wishes additional care, such as a polish change, an appropriate charge is added.

Skincare-based manicures and pedicures allow nail professionals wide choices in how they wish to conduct their businesses, plus support a welcome higher income, and increased professional respect.

Ancillary Services in the Nail Salon

Ancillary, according to Merrium-Webster Dictionary, picks up on the notion of providing aid or support in a way that supplements something else. In particular, the word often describes something that is in a position of secondary importance, such as the ancillary products in a company's product line," or in the case of salons, a service that is not the major focus of the salon.

Benefits of ancillary services

Ancillary services can provide benefits to the salon, such as the following:

1. Increasing the average ticket of the clients
2. Adding visits by current clients
3. Increasing the desire of clients to return/retention rate
4. Attracting new clients
5. Increasing the income of the professionals and the salon

Considerations in adding ancillary services

Ancillary services cannot be chosen via a whim. Nail salon owners must consider the following in the decision-making process:

Service "fit" - Adding ancillary services in a specialty salon must support the service focus. For example, an enhancement specialty salon is supported well by the more beauty-based services, such as nail art, makeup, and lashes while skin care-based services are supported well by treatment-based services, such as LED Light, paraffin, and facials. Others can be added and do well, of course, but consider these as "first adds."

Required license for the service – The provider of the new service must meet state requirements for licensure. Is a specific license needed to provide the service? Must a provider be hired just for the new service? Most times it is best to choose an existing employee who is properly licensed, train this provider(s) and then add the service. Keep in mind that a nail professional who is a licensed cosmetologist though specializing in nails can perform all services that are usually added in a nail salon.

Cost of equipment – Consider the cost of the physical set up and any needed ongoing purchases of equipment in the decision. Purchasing refurbished equipment is a good decision until the service is well established. Check out "used beauty equipment nearby" on search on the Internet and locations will come up.

Cost of products – Some services, such as waxing and paraffin – require few products; others, such as facials require many products that are higher in cost.

Space requirement – A minimal space requirement is preferred, but some ancillary services such as body message and facials require a room of their own. Unless a room is already available, this can be a major investment.

Plumbing and electrical requirements – These are major investments for a service. For example, a simple sink in a room is a major expense unless it is on the other side of a bathroom wall where the plumbing is just tapped into quickly and simply.

Training requirements – Some new services require little or even none, others require a lot, along with continuing upgrades in education. Know that clients can tell instinctively when a provider is not professionally trained.

Insurance requirements – Always check with your insurance company for coverage of every new service in your salon and add it to your coverage.

Marketing requirements – Marketing to current clients is always a given, but the amount of outside marketing that will be needed is also an important consideration. Do you need outside clients immediately to come in to make it profitable? Is the service new to the area? The new service to the area will require more marketing than one that is established. If the service is established in the area, the salon must market why going to this salon is a higher benefit to the clients.

Ancillary services for nail salons

Examples of these services include nail art, waxing, paraffin treatments, LED light treatments, arm and leg massage, lashes, reflexology and even facials and massage.

Nail art is a specialty that is included in our licensure and is an extremely popular add-on in many enhancement and natural nail salons. The complexity goes from stickers through free hand art and is according to management's definition of what can be offered and to the talent of the nail technician offering the skill. Many art specialties are available to offer but take training and experience – and talent – to offer them with success. The cost of adding the service varies from low (stickers) to extremely high, with the purchase of art supplies and equipment being a consideration,

Courtesy of Tom Truong, TomRTR Nails, Mesa, CA

Waxing license requirements vary from state to state. Some states allow nail technicians to wax clients to the knee or elbow; others have short courses for the addition of a waxing certification to a nail license; and others require a licensed esthetician or cosmetology professional perform the services. Investigate the requirements in the state you are working and perform this skill only according to state standards of practice. The cost of the addition of waxing services is low in that it may only include the wax pot, wax, and application sticks on a counter though some include a rolling cart to roll around the salon from station to station. In depth training is particularly important for the sake of safety and liability and is readily available by the manufacturers and at beauty shows.

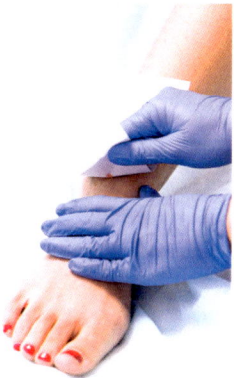

Makeup application requirements vary widely from state to state. A few states have no restrictions on makeup application; some have no restrictions but the client must perform the actual application to the skin, while others require the makeup artist is a licensed esthetician or cosmetologist. The wide variation indicates the salon must investigate the requirements at their state level. Many makeup companies offer training. The cost of adding makeup in a salon varies according to the setting the salon wishes to develop and amount of makeup products offered.

Paraffin services are included in nail technician licensure in all states and is a popular inclusion in high level spa and skin treatment care. An important consideration is the application method – infection control is an issue. No hands or feet should be immersed directly in the paraffin heat unit ever. Many methods exist for sanitary application and should be investigated and one appropriate for the salon chosen and trained. (See discussion later in this chapter.) The investment for this service is incredibly low, just the paraffin heater and the wax.

LED Light treatments can be performed by nail technicians and are a great addition to the services. These services can also be "drop in" services, meaning treatments for hyperpigmentation and anti-aging can suggest the client drop in for standalone LED treatments between the skin care-based treatments to enhance results. The standalone light must be purchased, but the lack of the need for professional support for the treatment can pay for the light quickly if the technicians encourage this ancillary service between their professional services. The client washes their hands and sits at a nail table for the LED treatment. The receptionist can set up the service in less than a minute and set the timer. Note: For enhanced results, place the hand on a platform of some type to get it closer to the lights.

Hand/Arm and Foot/Leg Massage can be a standalone treatment, though the salon must check the state laws. (Several states do not allow manicurists to massage, though they can apply lotion in a brief application massage.) The Foot/Leg Massage can be popular to those clients who stand on their feet a lot – the author had a teacher client who came in several days a week after school during the last weeks of school every year because she was outside monitoring the playground long hours for those relaxed play days of the year. The massage "fixed her up" every day on her way home from work!

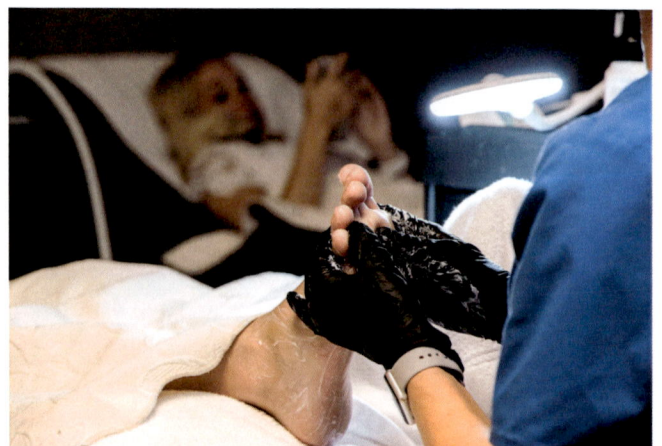

Lash services can be an ongoing income stream in a nail salon, though adding it as a service is according to state laws in the requirements of the provider. In every state, cosmetologists and estheticians can apply lashes, but many states also allow other licensees to take certification courses to enable them to perform this return-every-two-weeks service. The clients book them with their nail care, and they become an established service in their nail salon visit. Check the state SOP before investing. Lashes are inexpensive to set up in a salon, though most prefer to perform the service on a facial chair or tall makeup stool with a good stand up light which adds to the cost.

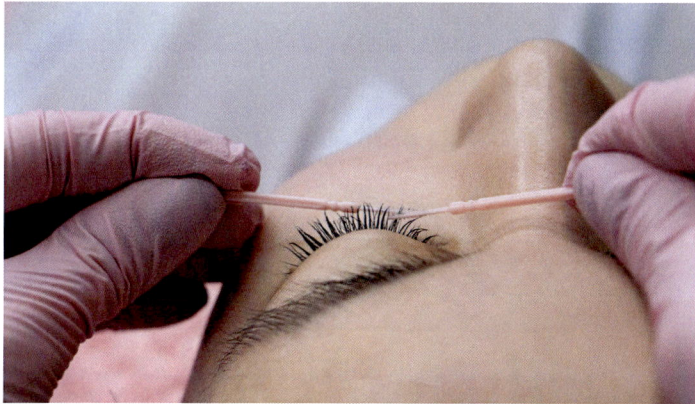

Reflexology – This specialty service is not well known but a good, well-trained Reflexologist can develop an ongoing clientele for this service. Check the laws in your state to ensure it is not restricted to massage therapists or requires a license or registration. Most of all, get excellent training by a certified trainer or the service will expose the short coming – reflexology clients can tell a difference immediately when a provider has had little training or a poor trainer.

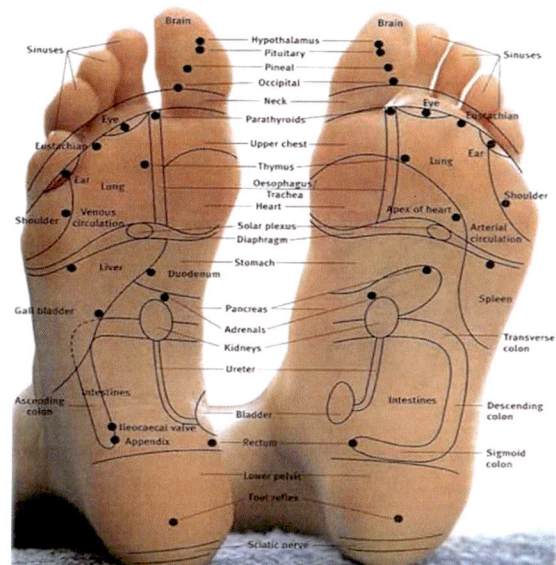

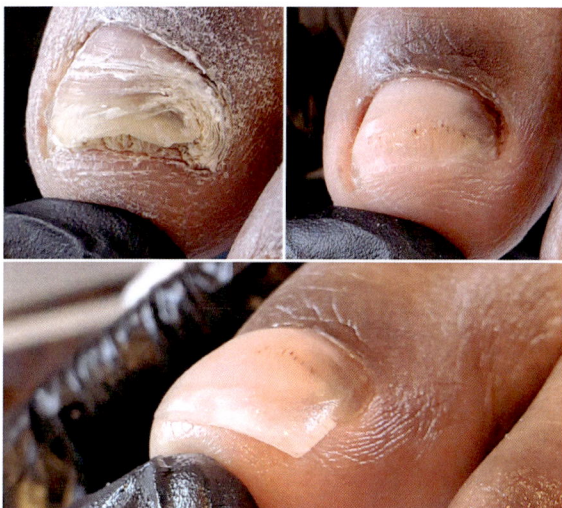

Toenail Restoration can be a highly sought after service from nail technicians who learn how to do them well - they are not "just like fingernails." Courses are available to learn their nuances. Most nail technicians performing the service charge $50 and up, according to their complexity of application. Podiatrists will refer their clients with damaged toenails to them.

Facials and massage services are offered in many nail salons, though they require the service provider is an esthetician or cosmetologist to perform facials, and a massage therapist for massages. Nail technicians cannot perform these services unless these licenses are added to their nail licenses. Also, they require a separate, quiet room, which can be challenging to provide in a nail salon. Facial rooms are expensive to set up – chair, light, steamer, many products, and much more – while the massage room is more basic, only requiring a massage table, blankets/towels, basic products, and a dimmer on the light switch.

This list of ancillary services is not complete as salons are continually developing new services to attract more clients. Investigate the service needs thoroughly prior to the investment in a new service. Do the set up and training well or do not add the service.

Chapter 9

Selling Home Care

Nail professionals have never liked selling, nor have they done much of it, saying, "I'm an artist, not a salesclerk." So, the median sales percentage for nail salons and nail departments in salons and spas the median sales percentage is a pitiful 7.5% (Kentley Insights, US. Nail Salons 2024). This low percentage suggests that many clients may need to ask to purchase an item, and products are seldom recommended by the nail professionals. It also indicates poor training in how to make recommendations. Additionally, some salons and spas may not offer products beyond nail polish, hand lotion, and a few fun items. This needs to change.

Many nail professionals perceive selling as "pushing products," and they often feel guilty about selling to clients who may not afford them. However, this perception is not accurate. The focus for all beauty professionals, including nail technicians, should be on meeting client needs. While it is acceptable to introduce fun products that might interest the client, the primary goal should be to recommend items that improve the skin and nails between services and enhance the results of professional treatments.

Nail Professionals extend their professional care through sending home care with their client.

To achieve this, nail professionals need a mindset shift. Instead of referring to these sales as "retail sales," they should be called "home care sales." This change in terminology can positively impact the way professionals approach selling. Alongside this shift, product knowledge training remains essential.

Comparing Retail and Home Care

The difference between retail and home care sales becomes evident when stated explicitly:

1. Retail items: These are products that clients pick up because they want them, not necessarily because they need them. Retail items cater to desires rather than specific needs.

2. Home care items: These are products needed to improve the nail's/skin's appearance or maintain service results. In home care sales, the focus is on meeting recognized needs.

The most significant distinction lies in the recommendation process. In home care sales, professionals recommend products that address specific client needs, such as improving or changing the skin or nails based on discussions during a service. Furthermore, home care items help maintain or extend the positive changes achieved during the service.

Education is Important

The low median sales percentage for nail salons and nail departments suggests nail professionals rarely recommend products. Inadequate training in product knowledge and sales techniques may contribute to this dismal sales performance.

Before incorporating professional and home care products into their services, nail professionals must thoroughly study the product ingredients. Understanding how each ingredient affects clients' skin is crucial. With the advent of recommendations in manicures and pedicures, effective home care becomes essential to achieve the desired results. Properly trained nail professionals recognize the potential of these new capabilities in meeting client needs and sell more, while increasing their income.

Home Care Sales Training

Effective training in home care sales is achievable, especially when professionals genuinely care about their clients' results and their own financial success. The training includes the following components:

1. Explaining the Difference: Retail vs. Home Care

- Nail professionals should understand that home care sales differ significantly from retail sales. While retail items cater to desires and impulse purchasing, home care items address specific needs and are recommended by trained professionals..

2. From "Pushing Products" to "Recommending"

- Professionals must shift their mindset from merely pushing products to making informed recommendations. The focus should be on meeting client needs.

3. Using the Sales/Results Chart

- Educate clients about the specific benefits of home care. Show them how these products enhance the results achieved during professional services. See Recommended Sales for the chart example.

4. Emphasizing Ingredient Knowledge

- Nail professionals should be well-versed in the ingredients of the products they recommend. This knowledge enhances customization of services and builds trust with clients. This information is available from the product manufacturers.

5. Client Retention and Growth

- Explain the importance of home care in maintaining client satisfaction and encouraging referrals. A client who sees positive results returns for services.

6. Encourage Client Education

- Teach professionals how to educate clients about their needs, correlate them with the product ingredients, and then train pros and clients in proper usage. Connect the recommended items with the targeted results to encourage purchase.

Let us put this another way. If few or none of nail professionals are at 15% in a salon, the owner needs to look at these responsibilities to see if management is meeting training requirements.

Recommendation Sales

In recommendation sales, professionals address specific client needs. For instance, they might recommend a treatment product for thin nails or an anti-pigmentation treatment for dark spots. The process involves educating the client on why the product is necessary, how its ingredients meet those needs, and how to use it effectively. This establishes a partnership between the nail professional and the client, developing a sense of shared responsibility. The client understands that using the recommended product at home maintains and extends the positive changes achieved during the service.

Home Care Compliance Report

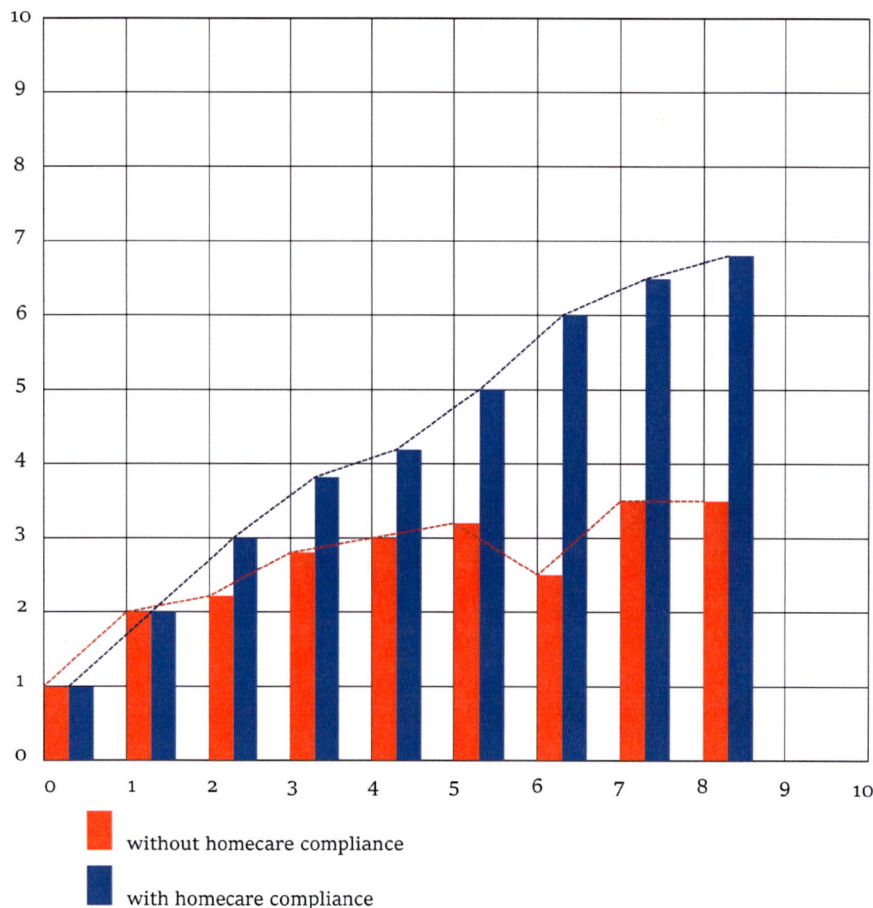

without homecare compliance

with homecare compliance

The Client Partnership

Focusing on "partnership" establishes the need to work together to achieve a stated goal and brings the client and professional together to enhance results. Following are the results of establishing this partnership:

1. Bond Building: A strong bond forms between the professional and the client, reinforced by visible results.

2. Client Referrals: Achieving goals with clients leads to word-of-mouth referrals and business growth.

3. Enhanced Reputation: The salon/spa and professionals gain a positive reputation through successful client partnerships.

Remember, consistently practicing this technique can significantly impact both the client's experience and the professional's success.

> **The Product Tells All...** It is crucial for professionals to consistently analyze and engage clients in discussions about improvements or maintenance. This ongoing dialogue cements the partnership over time and demonstrates genuine care for the client by the professional. Never cease the analysis step and asking questions.
> Sample question: "How much of the xx product do you have left?" Know this: most lotions and serums are packaged in 3-month amounts if consistently used. If a client has not finished the product within this time, it is likely they are not using it consistently. Similarly, if you notice lesser results, it may indicate non-compliance with recommended use. In such cases, a gentle prodding might be useful. Remember, this approach shows that you care and lessens the burden of results solely on the services. Use this opportunity to discuss the importance of partnership with the client.

Sampling: Introducing High-Quality Home Care Products

When nail professionals charge higher prices for results-oriented manicures and pedicures, they should also use and sell high-quality, results-oriented home care products. Consider offering a sample of an important product during the client's first appointment. Samples, available for purchase from product lines, should be large enough for at least five days of application. Five days is the usual when change becomes apparent when using skin care products. Clients must see a noticeable difference to be convinced to purchase when they return.

Selling and Success

Clients want their investment in services to last beyond the usual 48 hours. The key to achieving lasting results lies in taking home appropriate home care products, along with clear usage instructions. Failure to do so may lead to dissatisfaction with the service or the nail professional. Therefore, it is essential to recommend, explain, and sell home care products.

Measuring Success: Home Care Sales Percentage

Experts recommend that nail professionals working in salons or spas should aim to sell 15-20% of their production in home care products. Achieving this level of sales indicates excellent client retention and steady clientele growth. Simultaneously, the salon or spa itself thrives. Here is how to calculate the home care sales figure:

1. Choose a period of time (e.g., one month with twenty workdays).

2. Determine the dollars in sold home care products (e.g., $900).

3. Determine the dollars brought in through services (e.g., $6000).

4. Divide the service dollars into the home care sales dollars: $6000 / $900 = 15%.

Nail professionals selling less than 15% are usually not fully booked with requests as quickly as those achieving 20%. When home care sales are recommended and sold effectively, improvement is noticeable, client retention improves, loyalty grows, and the professional and salon or spa thrives. Home care sales are an important part of the Circle of Retention.

Nurturing Two Partnerships
Two partnerships should exist in this relationship:
1. Between the Nail Professional and the Client:
- A strong bond forms when both parties work toward mutual goals.
- Professional services and home care go hand in hand for lasting improvements.
- Gentle nudging and client education foster loyalty.
2. Between Professional Services and Home Care:
- The client's skin and nails improve significantly when both are aligned.
- Selling home care products is essential for success.
- The Circle of Retention ensures long-term client satisfaction.

Management's Responsibilities

The responsibility for achieving the desired home care sales percentage rests with management. To ensure nail professionals reach their potential in home care sales, client retention, and overall revenue, management must:

1. Expect Professionals to Sell:

- Set clear expectations that selling home care products is an integral part of the nail professional's role.

- Emphasize the importance home care has on results and client satisfaction.

2. Provide Training:

- Train professionals on effective selling techniques, including when and how to recommend products during service.

- Ensure professionals understand the benefits of home care for clients and the business.

3. Product Knowledge:

- Educate professionals about the ingredients in the products they recommend.

- Help them understand how each product addresses specific client needs.

4. Product Availability:

- Maintain a well-stocked inventory of important and appropriate home care products on the shelves.

- Ensure reordering processes are organized to prevent product shortages.

Most clients measure their services by their results, and home care can extend them much longer than if no home care is performed and enhance them. When results are extended, the client attributes them to the service provider's expertise, and client retention is amplified by these noticeable results. Making this happen is up to management.

If these conditions are not met within the spa or salon nail department, nail professionals may struggle to achieve their full potential. By aligning management practices with home care sales goals, both professionals and the business can thrive.

Chapter 10

Making Money in Manicuring and Pedicuring

A typical career track for licensed nail professionals can be outlined, although exceptions exist. It follows this trajectory:

1. Pre-Nail School:

- Individuals develop a passion for manicures, nails, art, and/or pedicures.

2. Nail School and Board Exam:

- Attend nail school to acquire the necessary basics for passing the board exam.

- Gain additional useful information and skills.

- Successfully pass the board exam.

3. First Salon Position:

- Begin working in a salon, focusing on training, experience, and public interaction.

- Many professionals move on from their initial job to explore other opportunities.

4. Career Development:

- Nail professionals fall in love with "doing nails" or specialize in a particular area of interest.

- New opportunities have transformed the nail industry, allowing professionals to pursue specialties beyond basic nail services.

Taking Control of Your Career

Every nail professional's journey is unique, but the key takeaway is that their career is entirely within their control. Personal decisions, such as where to work, what services to offer, and whether to specialize significantly impact their career. Waiting for a career to materialize without taking proactive steps rarely leads to reaching one's full potential. Those steps may include:

- Establishing the services most enjoyed – experience it all, but note the services preferred

- Education, education, and more education on the service(s) enjoyed

- Slowly narrowing the menu to the specialty-of-choice = specialization

New Opportunities for Specialization

In recent years, nail technicians' career potentials have improved significantly. The once-short career average in length of two years as recent as 2010 has changed due to a variety of new opportunities. Nail professionals can now make informed decisions about their ultimate specialty, which can dramatically enhance their income. Some of these opportunities include:

- Pedicures
- Nail Art
- Natural Nail Care
- Enhancements
- Specializing in working with the Chronically Ill and Elderly
- Collaborating with/working with Physicians or Podiatrists

  And many more

Many nail professionals are becoming specialists. For example, a nail professional chooses to specialize in natural nail care. In that case, they further refine their expertise by becoming highly educated and skilled as a "natural nail specialist," focusing exclusively on natural nails and skin care-based services. An even further specialty in natural nails is a pedicure specialty. A pedicure (pedicurist) specialist will focus on performing pedicures only. Upon achieving a clientele in their specialty, they no longer or rarely perform services outside their specialty.

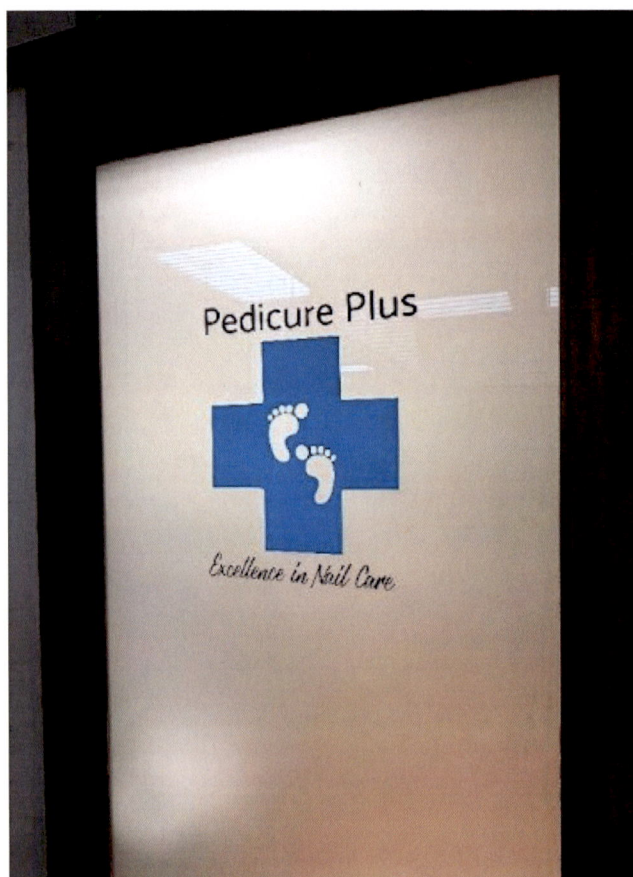

Specialties bring in loyal and respectful clients to nail professionals who put forth the effort required to become experts in one of their choosing.

Specialization: Becoming a Big Fish in a Small Pond

Most nail professionals aspire to be significant players rather than small contributors. How can you achieve this as a nail professional? By becoming indispensable to your clients and an essential part of their lifestyle. Specialization is a path to being the "go to" for clients in the professional's area of expertise.

Education is crucial when desiring to specialize. In this case, skin care-based services are the focus. But is education alone sufficient? To establish credibility, consider a step higher; obtain a certification related to your chosen specialty.

Certificates in the Nail Industry: Exhibiting Expertise

In all industries, certificates serve as markers of achievement and expertise through signifying advanced education. This is true in the nail industry also. Let us explore the different types of certificates in general and their marketing value in the nail industry:

1. Certificates of Attendance:

- Purpose: These certificates are either promotional (to attract new clients) or informational/skill-enhancing (for existing clients).
- Significance: While they indicate physical presence, they do not validate knowledge or skill acquisition.

Participations: These classes usually do not require participation in class activities, it is voluntary, if offered. Testing is not performed.

- Marketing Potential: Nail professionals may use the certificate for marketing, especially when attending trend-focused classes. However, many clients know the differences among certificates and do not value Certificates of Attendance.
- Payment: May or may not require payment.

2. Certificates of Completion:

- May or may not have pre-requisites, such as licensing,
- Significance: These certificates recognize competence achieved through required activities and testing.
- Participation Level: Professionals must meet specific participation requirements (e.g., project completion and/or exam success).
- Marketing Impact: Certificates of Completion demonstrate internalized knowledge and skill, making them valuable for marketing purposes.
- Payment: Usually requires payment for the course/testing and additionally for the certificate.

WELLNESS NAIL TECHNICIAN

Nailcare Academy, LLC

CERTIFICATE OF COMPLETION

is hereby granted to

To certify they have completed the Wellness Nail Technician Program to the satisfaction of Nailcare Academy, LLC and meets the highest standards of the Industry

Granted On

James McCormick MS, Co-Founder

Marketing a specialty Certificate is a technique which can bring in new clients and maintain a great clientele.

3. Competency-Based Certification

- Always has requisites, such as age and education levels, possibly pre-testing.

- Significance: Is the highest level: These credentials involve passing an examination based on a specific body of knowledge.

- Typical Use: Often used for licensing and competency-based certifications.

- Marketing impact: High level recognition of competency.

- Reassessments: May require reassessment of competence at specific time

- Payment: Requires payment by attendee for classes and testing. Separate payment for certificate or license .

Marketing Your Certifications

Announcing achievements can draw respect and new clients.

Marketing packets reward the nail professional for their efforts with new clientele.

- Display: Hang certificates prominently in your salon/spa.

- Elevator Speech: Develop a concise explanation of your specialty for every new clients and person's desired as collaborators.

- Marketing Materials: Include certifications in brochures and other marketing materials.

- Shelf Talkers: Place announcements near certificates and in the waiting room.

- Announce to Clients: Regular clients should be informed of new professional achievements, especially Certificates of Completion and Competency

- Online Presence: Highlight certifications on your website and social media.

- Press releases: A photo of the professional with an appropriate announcement attracts new clients and supports respect in regular clients.

Skin Care-Based Protocols can set you apart.
Skin care-based protocols can set you apart, whether as an add-on service alongside enhancements and other specialties or a core offering. To succeed, you must actively market these services to both existing and potential clients. Even before implementing changes, create anticipation by saying, "I'm upping my game in my favorite services by taking classes and am very excited about it! I cannot wait to show you!"

Manicuring & Pedicuring Mastery Certification

A Certificate of Manicuring and Pedicuring Mastery can be achieved through testing.

- This is Optional and there is a charge.

- How to Obtain: After reading this book, take the 50-question exam. See www.nailcareacademy.com/book for instructions.

- Benefits: Upon passing, download a free well-designed certificate to display.

- Marketing Opportunity: Announce the accomplished certification to clients and media and incorporate your accomplishment into your services, describing the difference.

Explaining certifications to new clients is a retention technique which brings rewards.

Marketing Strategies for Skin Care-Based Manicures and Pedicures

Effective marketing does not always require a big budget. In fact, personal, low-cost strategies often yield the most significant results. As you venture into skin care -based manicure and treatment-based pedicures, consider these tried-and-true methods to grow your clientele::

1. Claim Your Difference:

- Uniqueness Matters: Successful salons, spas, and studios can claim a special difference that sets them apart. For skin care-based services, this distinctiveness can be a powerful marketing tool.

- Announce It: Don't keep your new protocols a secret. Promote them to your existing clients and potential ones. Use phrases like, "We're taking advanced classes in skin and nail care to take our expertise to an even higher level!" And then announce the certification accomplishment to all who will listen.

2. Paper Announcements:

Even in these times, good ole paper and print marketing is successful to current clients.

- Flyers and Brochures: Provide informative flyers or brochures about your new services to every client. Receptionists should personally hand them out and explain their significance or they will be thrown away.

- Stand-Up Signs: Place attractive stand-up signs at the reception desk and other visible areas in your salon or spa. Tripods containing a picture of the professional and the announcement attractively done are very effective.

3. Leverage Social Media:

Media marketing can dramatically enhance success. Gaining or hiring these skills can announce a your "difference" to those who might not otherwise learn of an offered service.

- Before and After Pictures: Consistently post before-and-after pictures of your skin care-based manicures and pedicures on your social media accounts (with signed permission).

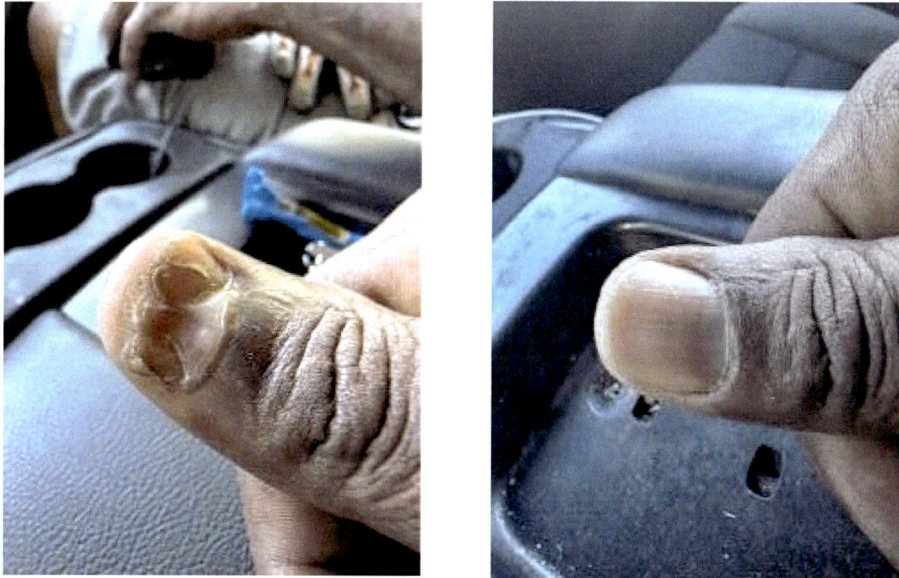

Before and after pictures are great marketing technique. Nail professionals who
focus on taking them see growth in clientele and client satisfaction. Pictures courtesy of WellNail.

- Testimonials: Share client testimonials to support the effectiveness of your new protocols. Actively collect with permission to use them.

- Learn from Others: Seek advice from successful nail professionals who have mastered social media marketing. They can guide you on best practices and mentor you toward success.

- Special Skills: Marketing the achievement of a special skill, such as the application of a prosthetic toenail from Nufeet Academy, Atlanta, Georgia, through media can attract new clients and expand ticket sales in a salon or spa.

Most clients measure their services by their results, and home care can extend them much longer than if no home care is performed. When results are extended, the client attributes them to the service provider's expertise, and client retention is amplified by these noticeable results.

Endorsement Marketing and the Value of Safety in Nail Services

1. Endorsement Marketing: Building Clientele

Endorsement marketing involves cross-promotion between professionals or departments within a salon or spa. By consistently referring clients to each other, professionals can quickly grow their clientele. However, structured referrals are essential:

- Open Discussion: Discuss referrals with other professionals.

- Specific Services: Clarify which services are in the referral process.

- Rewards: Determine any rewards (if applicable) for successful referrals.

- An agreement is established on time length, and benchmarks are established with numbers of referrals accomplished.

2. Marketing Packets: Reaching New Audiences

- Business Collaborations: Seek opportunities to include your information in marketing packets distributed by other businesses (e.g., bridal salons, real estate agencies, churches, large companies).

Call on companies to promote being included in their employee benefits package.

- Visibility: Ensure your information reaches potential clients who might not otherwise hear about you . Examples would be Senior Citizens organizations and business organizations. Independent living facilities love to listen to presentations.

3. The Value of Safety: Infection Control and Certifications

- Changing Landscape: Safety has become paramount due to concerns about infection transmission.

- Disinfection Product Certifications: Many companies offer certificates through courses on sanitation, disinfection, and safety.

    CJ's Centre for Beauty: Their Infection Prevention program provides comprehensive training and certification the staff can be required to take. The Certification becomes a marketing difference.

    Nailcare Academy, LLC: Offers online programs for Advanced Nail Technicians, Wellness Technicians, and Medical Nail Technicians, at www. nailcareacademy.com emphasizing safety and professional relationships with physicians and podiatrists. The certifications can become a marketing difference.

Marketing is a must, whether to current clients or in seeking new ones. When announcing a new service or change in focus, begin with your current clients before marketing to new ones.

Trending Manicures and Pedicures

These services can be "pop ups," meaning they come into our market from something that is trending on the internet or in society - suddenly they look great for a service in our salons, products are developed, and they are added either as a promotional service or placed on the menu. They can generate excitement that lasts or are just a flash in time – that aspect of trends is not controllable by the salon or industry. They just…happen, are there to stay forever to have a place on the salon menu or are gone in a short time, a thing of the past.

An example is the recent CBD trend. These manicures and pedicures sparked interest, full product lines were developed around them, products were developed within many established lines, and protocols were developed. Clients are attracted by their relaxation and pain relief results and salons are interested in their uniqueness. These services have become established now; most salons who offered them still do so, and they are on their salon menu.

When trends happen, investigate them thoroughly before jumping onto the band wagon. Following is a list of questions to ask and answer before investing.

Initial investment cost. Does the service require any new products or new equipment that only will be viable for that service?

Potential for profit. Is the number of potential new clients it will bring in high enough to invest? Or is the actual Return on Investment per service enough for the investment?

The demographic for the service. Is the number of people who will be interested large enough to gain a sufficient clientele for the service? To pay for products. Etc?

A one-time service, or initiates a return clientele. Is it a one-time services? If so, it must be higher in price to pay for the initial and ongoing investment. Potential for continual return clientele allows a loyalty factor to magnify profits.

Marketing. How much will it take and what kind? If the service is really new, it will need to have sufficient exposure to be successful.

Check legality. Are the professionals allowed to perform the service in your state? It must be within their scope of practice as listed in state regulations.

Insurance. Does the salon/professional's liability insurance policy cover the service? Some insurance companies are narrower than others in their coverable services list. Know for certain every service offered in the salon is covered.

Safety factors. Is the service fully safe for use on your clientele? Service safety must be thoroughly investigated. An example is the sudden appearance of "fish pedicures" in the US nail market several years ago. Many salons jumped on this trend without investigating the safety issues. Fish pedicures are now illegal in most states in the US because of their unsanitary water environment.

Education. How much education is needed for nail professionals to perform the service? Most trends require education of the professionals for successful launch and lasting success. To ignore this important part of the treatment addition can be a mistake for salons.

Trends are fun, but responsible professionals and salon owners must look past their initial intense spark of interest into defining how they fit into the clientele and into the financial aspects of their business. And in how long they may last as a viable service.

Are skin care-based manicures and pedicures going to be a permanent upgrade to nail care menus? These services are expansions of techniques and enhance the results of current services, allowing the nail professionals a higher level of respect from clients, a higher level of loyalty, and higher profits. With proper preparation, including education and high-quality products, these services have earned their permanent placement on nail care menus.

Conclusion

Achieving Success in Skin Care-Based Manicures and Pedicures

In this journey toward success, nail professionals have explored skin care-based manicures and pedicures, discovering their transformative potential for their clients and their career. Let us recap the key takeaways:

1. Expanding Within Current Services:

- Nail professionals can enhance their offerings by incorporating the concept of skin care-based treatments into their skills.

- Skin care-based services focus on meeting the needs of clients.

- The quality of the partnership between the nail professional and the client is important to the results of the care and the development of loyalty.

- The amount of client commitment to home care can enhance or diminish the results of the care.

2. Potential for Dropping External Marketing:

- Internal marketing becomes the focus of the extraordinarily successful nail professional.

- When the "schedule ceiling" is met, successful professionals focus on their tried-and-true clients through accepting only their personal referrals to fill their rare opening, allowing their loyalty to be cloned.

- Becoming essential in clients' lifestyles is achievable through specialized services.

- 85% to 90% booked allows income expansion through raising prices on an ongoing basis for successful professionals.

3. Passion, Knowledge, and Commitment:

- True success lies within these characteristics of the nail professional.

- Passion, continuous learning, genuine care for clients, and pride in results drive high achievement.

- Committing to obviously superior customer care and professionalism can enhance success to its full potential.

4. Tools for Success:

- The protocols provided here empower passionate, knowledgeable, and caring nail professionals.

- The expansion of knowledge necessary for effectively performing skin care-based services can support nail professionals to a new level of care for their clients.

- Acknowledging the importance of home care in professional nail care is a game changer.

- Commitment to client needs leads to client satisfaction and higher income.

- Acquiring certifications with the purpose of expanding knowledge and skills can become a marketing positive for nail professionals.

- The nail professional demonstrating through certifications the expansion of their expertise has continual career growth and success.

Incorporating the information in Manicuring and Pedicuring Mastery into career skills takes a nail professional to a higher level of care and income.

Appendix

Contents

Beyond the Basics: Manicure/Pedicure Protocols for the Skincare-Based Manicurist/Pedicurist

The following protocols are designed for *Manicuring and Pedicuring Mastery* as treatment manicures/pedicures as well as relaxing ones. They are new protocols, different than those taught in the schools as they bring the massage treatment to earlier in the service to warm the skin, allowing the treatment products to penetrate earlier in the service and thus, to be more effective. With the massage in this location in the protocol, it also relaxes the client earlier and longer in the service. Several manicures/pedicures are listed.

Soakless (or No-Soak, Dry, Waterless) – This pedicure/manicure is designed for clients who cannot soak their feet. It is relaxing and appropriate for everyone. The manicure/pedicure can be any of the following.

The Basic – This manicure/pedicure is the base treatment from which all these services are designed.

The Scrub – This manicure/pedicure is for dry and flaky hands/feet to open the skin to treatment.

The Relaxation/Hydration – This manicure/pedicure hydrates the hands/feet while being the ultimate in relaxation. It is the most hydrating pedicure of all.

The Callus Control – This manicure/pedicure is designed to reduce calluses over time, without blades. It is performed as a monthly service or in a program/series with treatments performed alternate weeks between services.

The Anti-Aging/Hyperpigmentation – This manicure/pedicure reduces appearance of aging (fine lines and wrinkles) and can be upgraded to also reduce hyperpigmentation.

Pedicure/Manicure Equipment, Supplies and Home Care

The set up for a service is important for defining functionality and client comfort. Listed are the basics for performing a full menu of manicures/pedicures. The list is not all-inclusive, but will get a technician on the track to performing the services well.

Basic Equipment

- Nail Professional and client chairs
- Paraffin set up (aseptic method)
- Drying chair area (Optional)
- Stainless Steel implements
- E-File/bits (preferably portable)
- Gloves (Nitrile)
- Towels
- Nail/Foot wash brushes
- Cabi (Optional)
- Ultrasonic Cleaner (Optional)
- LED Treatment Light (Optional)
- LED Gel Light (Optional)
- Autoclave (target for Safe Salon)

Supplies

- Disposable Files, nail and callus
- Lint-free polish removal pads
- 2x2s
- Pure Acetone Polish Remover
- Polish/base/topcoat
- Disposable files and Pedi-Paddles
- Disposable implements/supplies
- Disinfectant and cleaning products/set up
- Autoclave maintenance supplies
- Autoclavable/disinfectable tongs

Home Care Products

- Lotions
- Anti-Fungal Lotion
- Resurfacing Lotion (low %)
- Moisturizing Lotion
- Hyperpigmentation Lotion
- SPF Lotion (with Hydration)
- Scrub Product (Gentle)
- Treatment Products
- Home Care Instructions
- Files, etc.
- Polish/basecoat/topcoat

Professional Treatment Products

- Foot Scrub Product
- Healing Massage Lotion
- SPF Lotion
- Polish
- Basecoat/topcoat
- Regular polish
- Lasting polish (Gel, DazzleDry and/or CND Shellac)
- Antifungal
- Treatments and Masks

What nail professionals utilize in their craft is individual choice. Everyone is unique in their choices. This list is basic and general but provides a new skin care-based nail technician a list to start from in beginning these special treatments.

New Client Sheet

For us to serve you at our very best, we need to know you better.
Please fill out the following information.
Thank you.

Date_____
Name_____ Occupation_____
Is this your first time to our salon?_____ If so, how did you hear about us? _____
_____
Address_____City/State/Zip_____
Preferred Contact telephone number_____ Email_____
Have you ever had a pedicure before?_____ If so, when was your last pedicure_____

General Health
Are you currently on any medications? _____ If so, for what reason?_____
_____
Are you currently under a physician's care?_____ If so, please discuss this with your technician in detail.
Are you pregnant? _____If so, how many months?_____ Do you smoke? _____

Please circle any medical problems you have or have had: Are you using/taking:

Blood Pressure (Low or High)	Kidney problems	Antibiotics
Cold hands and feet	Tuberculosis	Hormones/HRT
Varicose Veins	Anemia	Blood Thinners
Arthritis, Tendinitis, Bursitis	Hepatitis A, B, C	Chemotherapy
Cancer	Diabetes (1 or 2)	Skin Treatment
Circulatory problems	Fibromyalgia	
Heart problems	Stroke	
Stress related illness	Thyroidism (Hyper, Hypo)	
HIV/AIDS	Scoliosis	
Osteoporosis	An Autoimmune disease	
Skin disease of any kind	COVID	

Pedicure Services:
Are your feet comfortable in shoes?_____Do you have any pain in your feet?_____
If so, where? _____
Do your feet sweat? _____ Do you have excessive calluses? _____
If so, where? _____
Are your nails healthy? Dry? Brittle?_____ Do your feet swell?_____
Do you have any foot problems the Medical Nail Technician should know about?_____
If so, what are they?_____

All appointments are guaranteed by a credit card. If you cancel an appointment 24 hours or more before the appointed time, no charges will be added to your card. Not coming to an appointment with no notice preventing others from scheduling at that time will result in a XX% charge to the card of the service for which you were scheduled.
Signature_____ Date_____

Basic Soakless Technique

This client can be sitting or lying back; must be comfortable. All pedicure/manicure implements are still in the sterilization pouch or wrapped neatly in a towel, lying on a clean table or pedicure stand along with other supplies. **Most basic services do not include the legs/arms in the service.**

1. The new client health information is filled out pre-service. Seat him/her according to policies and discuss the health sheet contents. **Put on gloves. Check the sheet for contraindications to having a service.** If not appropriate, refer him/her to a podiatrist or dermatologist and perform a placating service.

2. **Analysis. Examine the feet/hands and discuss conditions with the client.** Next, remove polish, then check the condition of the nails/shorten and shape them. Suggest services now, if different than scheduled treatment. Adjust suggestions according to the health responses and conditions of the skin/nails. If needed, the dry callus exfoliation is performed now.

3. **Cleanse**. Wet the feet/toes with a warm, wet towel and then apply a gel/foam cleanser, massaging it around the area for 1-2 minutes. Use a gentle, obvious massage technique. Remove any residual. **Cover/wrap the foot/hand while not being treated with a towel.** Perform on the second foot/hand.

4. **Scrub/Exfoliation.** Apply a scrubbing product to the first foot/hand, rub gently into the skin, more so into the calluses. Use effleurage movements. Spend no more than 1 minute on the exfoliation. Remove with a warm, wet towel, dry and then cover with a dry towel. Perform on the second foot/hand, cover.

5. **Massage**. Apply massage product and perform the appropriate massage on the first foot/hand. Next, apply the eponychium treatment and the callus treatment, then wrap in a towel and set aside. Perform on the second foot/hand. (Never leave the callus treatment on longer than recommended.)

6. **Callus Treatment.** Remove the cover, etc., from the first foot/hand, remove the callus treatment with a wet cloth, and perform the callus exfoliation with a pedi-paddle or a pedicure bit on an e-file

7. **Eponychium (Cuticle) Treatment.** Remove TX product and perform treatment. After, wrap the foot/hand in a dry towel, and lay aside. Now move to the second foot/hand, repeat.

8. **Polish Prep.** For feet, apply toe separators or put on sandals. Replace jewelry and coat, then cleanse nails with dehydrant.

9. **Polish.** Discuss the home care and retrieve the products. Discuss/make next appointment, then polish.

10. **Close.** Make next appointment and provide a card, clean and reset the treatment area for the next client. Prepare implements, place in a pouch/in the autoclave or into disinfectant, fill out records.

Basic Soakless, Short Form

1.) Dry exfoliation, (optional), overall observation and cleansing massage
2.) Skin analysis, remove polish, nail analysis, shorten, shape
3.) Recommendations
4.) Exfoliation massage/removal, then relaxation massage. Apply cuticle softener.

Mask and treatment products are added here for higher level services

5.) Apply callus softener, perform cuticle removal (nail plate), eponychium grooming, then callus work
6.) Polish prep and polish
7.) Home care instruction, reappointment, and release

Suggestion: Learn where you must be on the service clock with each skill to be on time. Then you can check during the service where you are in the protocol to know what you must do to see your next client on time.

Suggestion: Learn to know when the feet will take too much time for you to see your next client on time. If it will take too much – usually callus work or grooming of thickened, too long nails, explain the appointment is going to take more time than you have and why and make a "treatment appointment." Explain the second appointment will not include polishing. (Provide price. The amount is dependent on what must be done.)

The Scrub Pedicure/Manicure Procedure

The Scrub Pedicure/Manicure is designed to treat rough and scaly skin on the feet/hands or to "open" dry skin to treatment. Treating the legs/arms additionally is an upgrade. Time allotted will be 45 minutes to one hour, according to the condition of the skin and the policies of the salon/spa.

Basic Soakless with an Enhanced Exfoliation

Apply a scrubbing product to the first foot/hand and rub gently into the skin, more so into the calluses. Use obvious effleurage movements and spend no more than 2 minutes per foot/hand on the exfoliation massage. Remove with a warm wet towel, dry, and then cover with a dry towel. Perform the same procedure on the second foot/hand.

Scrub Pedicure/Manicure Protocol Description

1. Entrance and seating.

2. Foot/hand/nail analysis and recommendations

3. Cleanse massage.

4. Enhanced exfoliation massage.

5. Foot massage.

6. Callus treatment.

7. Eponychium treatment.

8. Prep for polish/finish

9. Polish/drying procedure.

10. Appointment "close" procedures. Prep/reset for next client.

Deluxe Scrub Pedicure for Feet and for Dry Scaley Legs/Arms

The legs/arms are only included if the client asks or it can be suggested by the professional during analysis. Many will want a scrub to alleviate dry legs/arms – approximately 1 minute on each leg. The pedicure should take a few more minutes though many professionals can add it within the regular time of the service.

This upgrade increases the cost of the treatment so the price should be higher. After the exfoliation, each leg/arm is wrapped in a towel (warmed, if possible, not wet) to enhance penetration and moisturizing during the remaining treatment.

The Hydrating/Relaxation Protocol

The Hydrating or Relaxation Manicure/Pedicure is an upgraded version of the Scrub Pedicure/Manicure plus a hydrating mask and is a procedure designed specifically for dry skin or as a relaxing pedicure. It can be an upscale specialty manicure/pedicure if a relaxation treatment and more is incorporated into those offered (The Spa Manicure/Pedicure, Themed Manicure/Pedicure).

High-end spa services will contain amenities. These services may include paraffin, aromatherapy neck pillows, specialty drinks and other relaxing amenities/treatments to become "spa." The service usually includes the leg/arm so takes longer and the price is higher. Take care in pricing to keep it profitable by costing the products and the additional time.

This Service is the Basic Soakless with #4, Exfoliation/Scrub and #5, the Massage, and includes the legs and arms.

#4, Exfoliation/Scrub. Dead cells accumulate on the surface of the skin and must be removed and disrupted.

#5. Massage and Treatment. The Massage Lotion is applied, and appropriate massage technique is performed. The callus and eponychium treatment products are applied, post massage, and then the foot is wrapped neatly in a towel (a dry, slightly warmed one, if possible) and laid aside to allow the products to penetrate. The procedure is completed on the second foot.

Remove the callus and eponychium products and perform the hydrating treatments, such as a mask, a mask plus paraffin, and other hydrating care.

Hydrating/Relaxation Manicure/Pedicure Protocol Description

1. Entrance and seating.

2. Foot/hand/nail analysis and recommendations

3. Cleanse massage.

4. Exfoliation massage.

5. Foot massage.

Additional treatment and relaxation, according to salon protocols

6. Callus treatment.

7. Eponychium treatment.

8. Prep for polish/finish

9. Polish/drying procedure.

10. Appointment "close" procedures. Prep/reset for next client.

Hydrating <u>Treatment</u> Description

This reduced time and protocol version of this manicure/pedicure is performed weekly between the bi-weekly manicures and bi-weekly between monthly full pedicures for treatment of dry skin. Usually, the treatments can be reduced to the bi-weekly manicures and the monthly pedicure within a few treatments if <u>the home care is performed as recommended</u>. The treatment will take 20 minutes-half hour, according to expertise of the professional.

The price is less than the full service – possibly is at about 60% of the full service. Note that the exfoliation step is important in hydrating services to prepare the skin for the ingredient penetration. Always discuss the needed home care compliance.

- Seating of the client.

- Cleanse the foot/hands.

- Exfoliate the treatment area.

- Apply the mask to both feet/hands, leave the required time. then remove.

- Reappointment and release (no polish).

- Infection Control of the area.

Some clients want or need a paraffin treatment – the price goes up, as does the time. Additional services, such as a polish change or paraffin, increase the price.

The Callus Control Pedicure/Manicure and Treatment

This treatment is designed to reduce and/or control calluses on the feet/hands. It has two forms, the pedicure/manicure, and the treatment. The treatments do not include aesthetics such as polishing, and the amount of time is shorter than the usual service. This service reduces the incidence of infections and heavier calluses through the use of blades and post-treatment is painless when performed properly. It may also be a monthly maintenance pedicure on a high callus-producing client to reduce the incidence of calluses.

Callus Control Manicure/Pedicure Protocol Description

1. Entrance and seating.

2. Client, analysis and recommendations, polish removal.

3. Cleanse, shorten shape.

4. Exfoliation Massage.

5. Massage, if any. Product applications, set time.

6. Remove products. Callus care performed.

7. Eponychium treatment care.

8. Nail bed cleansing/Post Appointment procedures.

9. Polish/finish.

10. Close, cleaning and Re-set. Record keeping.

Callus Control Treatment Protocol Description

- Entrance and seating.
- Cleanse.
- Exfoliation massage. Apply callus softener product, wrap in towel, allow to sit the required time.
- Remove well with wet towel and perform callus reduction.
- Apply lotions.
- Reappointment.
- Close. Reset. Record.

Any additional service is an extra charge.

PRECAUTIONS/COMMENTS for Callus Pedicure and TX:

Calluses must be closely monitored especially on persons with slow healing possibilities due to the potentials for ulcers developing beneath them.

Pay close attention to the set time for the callus softener as per the product instructions. Do not allow to go beyond that. Remove prior to exfoliation.

Re-evaluate for progress for exfoliation at the start of every tx appointment. End the series at point of proper achievement. The number of treatments is according to severity.

Remember that some callus must remain until the causative is removed.

Post series, this client returns to the Callus Control Pedicure as monthly maintenance.

Anti-Aging/Hyperpigmentation Protocol

These are treatment services in a series; one-service-only does not produce the results the client seeks. These are new to most manicurists and pedicurists and should be studied well before use. Know the precautions.

Anti-Aging and Hyperpigmentation Service Protocol Description

1. Entrance and seating.

2. Client foot/hand analysis and recommendations, polish removal.

3. Cleanse, shorten shape.

4. Exfoliation massage, then foot/hand massage, if any. Product treatment application, with set time.

5. Callus care

6. Eponychium treatment care.

7. Nail bed cleansing/polish prep.

8. Appt procedures

9. Polish/finish.

10. Cleaning and Re-set. Record keeping.

Anti-aging and Hyperpigmentation Treatment Protocol Description

- *Entrance and seating.*
- *Cleanse.*
- *Exfoliation massage, if any. Application of treatment product.*
- *Full removal of treatment product followed by the care.*
- *Apply lotion, including SPF and Lightening products.*
- *Reappointment.*
- *Close and reset.*

PRECAUTIONS/COMMENTS for Anti-Aging and Hyperpigmentation Care:

MASSAGE IS MINIMAL OR NONE, according to the sensitivity of the skin and the products used. Massage increases the depth of the penetration for treatment AHAs, which can be dangerous.

Choice of anti-aging and hyperpigmentation products are very important. Exfoliant products and lighteners are always used as directed.

15-20% AHA lotions are applied and lightly massaged into the skin during treatment. Liquid AHAs are brushed on with a facial brush and allowed to set. Remove both with a cool, wet towel and apply a hydrating lotion. No massage is performed when liquid exfoliators are used in the service.

Actively monitor the client's skin during the treatment for redness and sensitivity. Remove the product well with a cool, wet towel and neutralize immediately with cool water, if any redness or stinging occurs.

Anti-aging treatments begin at 2 minutes per treatment, with time added each service. Never go past 5-7 minutes per treatment even for the strongest of skin.

Homecare use of SPF and lighteners is very important/required. Use of low percentage anti-aging home care products is also important to maintain sloughing of dead cells.

Exposure to the sun cancels the potentials to reach goals and re-introduces the prior problem very quickly.

Anti-aging and hyperpigmentation produce slow though obvious progress and results. Before and After pictures are necessary.

Light Therapy

The use of UV light in treatments can enhance results with no addition of side effects. The light enhances cellular activity in anti-aging and anti-hyperpigmentation care. Utilize the light after the treatments also as this reduces inflammation and hyper responses.

Standalone lights allow the light therapy to be performed after the appointment, even after the polish has been applied, adding no time to the appointment schedule.

In-treatment with hand-held Light Therapy adds time to the appointment, 10 minutes to each hand. (Using two lights reduces this time.)

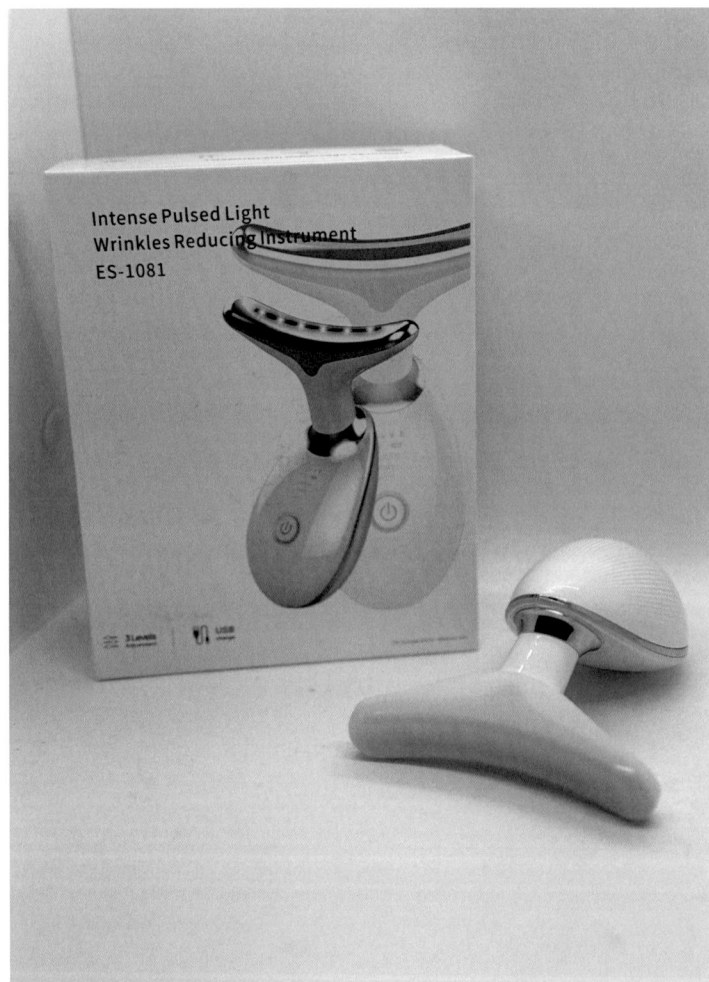

OSHA in Nail Salons

OSHA's Bloodborne Pathogens standard, 29 CFR 1910.1030, requires employers to evaluate whether an employee (any employee) may encounter blood or other potentially infectious material. If this risk exists, then the employer must follow the requirements of the standard, including providing training, vaccination, and personal protective equipment – gloves.

Go to OSHA.gov to read what OSHA says about nail salons and the exposure of employees to hazards on that site. The standard's requirements state what employers must do to protect workers who are occupationally exposed to blood or other potentially infectious materials (OPIM), as defined in the standard. That is, the standard protects workers who can be anticipated to encounter blood (or OPIM) because of doing their job duties. The booklet from OSHA, *Stay Healthy and Safe while Performing Manicures and Pedicures* educates nail technicians on safety issues in the salon. On page 12, Biological Hazards has a full discussion concerning the need to wear gloves in salons as stated in the 2001 updated OSHA Standards.

The fact that some employers ignore OPIM and do not require gloves does not take the responsibility of self-protection off the individual technician. If the employer does not see the need, this decision is left as totally the responsibility of the individual technician.

Question? Do you feel a nail professional might on some occasion be exposed to blood or some other potentially infectious material during their performance of manicures and pedicures or other services on their clients? If so, PPEs (Personal Protective Equipment) must be worn while performing these services.

Statement from Janet McCormick: I know this is discussed widely in our industry, so I will provide my opinion.

Do not be careless or ignorant of the facts of our service exposures. Facts are facts. We are potentially exposed to blood – with little doubt, every nail technician who has worked on clients for more than a few weeks has been exposed to blood and is past the "potential" standard. Knowing this, you can decide to wear gloves as protection from any potential exposure as OSHA dictates per OPIM. Beyond that, many infections are contagious 24-48 hours prior to their obvious symptoms on the client, example, digital herpes.

Many technicians consider their state's "blood spill" protocol in their decision on wearing gloves. If you are comfortable with cleaning up blood as sufficient protection, that is your decision. (We all have watched CSI and seen the "left overs" from blood – even a drop.) But it is not according to OSHA standards.

Consider this, also: clients make judgements according to their information and they are no longer ignorant of the protection gloves offer since COVID…and their nail technician wearing gloves may be among their requirements. I am one of them. No gloves, you do not work on me. But I also understand that wearing gloves requires "glove rules," and that wearing them does not clearly indicate a "safe nail technician." (The rules must be followed…) But it is a step in the right direction.

Make an informed decision – yes or no to gloves – and move on. Take care of yourself and feel comfortable with your decision. But know this. Being argumentative about it means you have doubts about your decision. So, again, decide, and that is it! Be quiet, professional, and move on, whatever you decide. Then, be prepared to back up your decision when clients ask about your stance. A few will ask and they have a right to a quiet, professional and factual answer.

Most everyone in our industry has been given the facts and most have made their own decision. And it may be different than yours. Know this: Arguing rarely changes anyone's mind, so refuse to do it. Stop arguing about gloves with closed minded people! It only produces animosity that is unnecessary. And from there, it's simple: the clients will decide on whether to stay or leave by their own values.

Recommended Products

This author realizes there are few products for nail technicians to purchase in the nail industry for skin care-based services, and for that reason, is stepping out of the norm and listing some that currently working for skin care-based manicurists/pedicurists successfully.

This list will evolve as products are developed, and the list will be placed on www.nailcareacademy.com under About/Links and Resources and will change over time. Check it out occasionally for new additions that have been vetted for their benefits.

The products are listed alphabetically.

BS Brace

A non-surgical treatment to correct nails with extreme curvatures or are ingrown. A strip across the nail produces a gentle lifting bringing the nail back into the side walls and to a normal curvature.

https://cjscentreforbeauty.com)

CND Shellac

A long-lasting gel polish once, cured in the CND LED Lamp, results in 14+day high-shine finish that dries instantly and is resistant to smudging. When it is time to remove, the polymers quick release the coating from the nail in a tidy, efficient, and safe way.

https://www.cnd.com/pages/find-a-distributor

Dazzle Dry

Long lasting. Quick drying. Nontoxic. No UV. Vegan nail care formulated in Chandler, Arizona , a great non-damaging. long lasting coating for nails. A direct purchase product.

https://dazzledry.com

Footlogix

Restorative skin and foot care products. Sign up for their newsletter to learn about their monthly free education. Footlogix - ANT Class Certificate holders get 10% off all Footlogix products!

https://Footlogix.com

IBX Nail Treatment

A penetrating, restorative two part system for strengthening damaged nails, developed by Famous Name, Las Vegas NV. A diret purchase product.

https://famousnamesproducts.com/the-ibx-system/

WellNail

A soothing, strengthening balm for damaged, weak nails to promote healing and growth toward becoming beautiful and healthy nails. This company is developing a full line of products for skin care-based nail technicians.

https://wellnail.net

www.ingramcontent.com/pod-product-compliance
Lightning Source LLC
Chambersburg PA
CBRC090850210326
41597CB00008B/160